Spelling

Approaches to teaching and assessment

Spelling

Approaches to teaching and assessment

Peter Westwood

 **David Fulton** Publishers

First published 1999 as
Spelling
by Australian Council for Educational Research Ltd
19 Prospect Hill Road, Camberwell, Victoria, 3124

Published in Great Britain (with amendments) in 2004 by
David Fulton Publishers, 414 Chiswick High Road, London W4 5TF

10 9 8 7 6 5 4 3 2 1

British Library Cataloguing-in-Publication Data
A catalogue record for this book is available from the British Library

ISBN 1 84312 193 X

Printed in Great Britain

Contents

Preface

This book provides an overview of some of the effective ways of helping students to develop and improve their spelling skills. The emphasis throughout the text is on the importance of explicit teaching. Many of our students need to be taught appropriate strategies for word study, and for editing and checking their own spelling. Students do not necessarily acquire these strategies through incidental learning. Research has supported the view that spelling skills can be improved by carefully structured intervention.

Assessment is seen as an essential aspect of the effective teaching of spelling. It is important that teachers can determine how far an individual student has come on the path from beginning speller to independence. The formal and informal approaches to assessment described in the second half of this text will enable teachers to determine the instructional needs of individuals.

I have resisted the strong temptation to include a section containing word lists constructed according to visual, phonic or morphemic principles. When such lists are provided, they tend to be adopted by teachers as the prescribed 'spelling curriculum', rather than used as a resource into which they might dip selectively to meet the needs of specific students. If teachers require such lists, they are to be found in many of the resources listed in the final section of this book.

I wish to thank Dr David Moseley for permission to reproduce his core list of common spelling errors which first appeared in the text *The Psychological Assessment of Reading*, edited by J. R. Beech and C. Singleton (London: Routledge, 1997). My thanks also to the Department for Education, Training and Employment in South Australia for permission to reproduce the South Australian Spelling Test (1993) which appears as an Appendix in the resource book *Spelling: From Beginnings to Independence*, published by the Department in 1997. I am grateful for the assistance of Lee-Anne Benson and Meredith Poulson in the preparation of tables and figures for this book.

PETER WESTWOOD

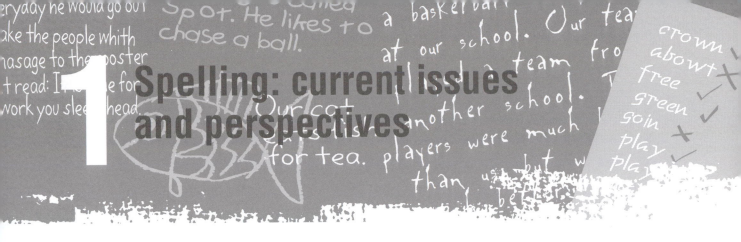

> Spelling is a tool for writing. The purpose of learning to spell is so that writing may become easier, more fluent, more expressive, and more easily read and understood by others. (Gentry & Gillet 1993, p. 57)

In precisely the same way that the teaching of grammar in schools 'incites an enormous amount of active and sharp debate' (Candlin 1997, p. 5), so too the teaching of spelling is an issue that arouses strong emotions in both parents and teachers. Almost everyone has strong views about the importance (or lack of importance) of accurate spelling. The focus in the contemporary debate concerns the question of whether spelling skills are best learned naturally and incidentally through the process of engaging in authentic writing across the school curriculum, or whether specific time and effort should be devoted to the direct and explicit teaching of spelling skills and strategies (Clark & Uhry 1995). A perspective is emerging now that a well-balanced *combination* of these two approaches is required to ensure that all students have the opportunity to become proficient spellers (Butyniec-Thomas & Woloshyn 1997).

How important is spelling?

One viewpoint is represented by those educators who argue that when students write, the ideas they attempt to convey and the quality of the language they use are far more important considerations than any accuracy in spelling. It is sometimes suggested that to place too great an emphasis on accuracy in spelling may even inhibit children's willingness to write. Under this condition most of their mental effort has to be directed toward the lower-level cognitive process of encoding each word correctly, rather than to the higher-order processes involved in generating new ideas and expressing these in an interesting written form (Huxford, McGonagle & Warren 1997). There is a great deal of common sense in this viewpoint, particularly in the context of the writing of very young children. One would not want to impede the creative aspects of their earliest attempts at writing by forcing them to concentrate from the start on correct spelling. Too much attention to accuracy can undermine a child's motivation to engage in writing. For example, Lowe and Walters (1991) described a 12-year-old boy, Darren, who found it extremely difficult to begin any piece of writing because he was frightened of making a mistake. There may be many other reluctant writers like Darren in our classrooms. Their self-esteem and confidence in relation to their writing ability are often impaired due to early criticism of their work by parents, peers or teachers (Gentry & Gillet 1993; Leary & Johncock 1995).

An alternative viewpoint considers that learning to spell accurately is extremely important and that direct teaching from an early stage is necessary in order to help students master spelling principles. It is argued that an individual's literacy level is often judged by others in terms of his or her ability to spell words correctly in everyday written communications, such as in letters, notes, reports and application forms. Parker (1991) has remarked:

> In our society, being a proficient speller is important. Good spelling is regarded as the mark of a 'well-educated' person, and because of this it can affect a child's future opportunities and choices in life. (p. 64)

Poor spelling can impede a student's academic performance in a variety of ways. For example, inaccurate spelling reduces intelligibility of written work, and conveys to others the impression that the writer is either careless or less intelligent than other students (Stewart & Cegelka 1995). This is a serious problem for students who are, for example, genuinely dyslexic. Thomson (1995) reports that in many schools, colleges and universities the written work of intelligent students with dyslexia is frequently misjudged and undervalued due to the large number of spelling errors it contains.

If spelling is so important for communication purposes, how should it be taught in schools? How can teachers balance the conflicting demands of having to aim for steady improvement in children's spelling skills while at the same time allowing the children the freedom to take risks and to experiment in their writing? What has research had to say about normal acquisition of spelling skills, and about specific difficulties in learning to spell? What should children be taught in order to become more proficient spellers? These issues will be addressed in the following pages.

Approaches to spelling instruction

Twenty-five years ago 'spelling' often appeared as a specific lesson on the timetable of many primary schools. Teachers used this time to provide the students with weekly spelling lists, often based on the new vocabulary that had emerged from the various topics and themes studied within the week, or sometimes based on specific 'word families' sharing common sequences of letters. The time was also used to check that the students knew the meanings of the words and could use them appropriately in sentences. A weekly test was often administered to ensure that the words had been memorised correctly by the children (Rowe & Lomas 1996). Frequent use was made of such resources as spelling lists, or of word lists published by the government education departments. In addition, children were usually required to correct the errors they made within essays and other forms of written work, and were expected to write each correction several times for additional practice.

This approach had a certain appeal to it. It was systematic. Children knew what was expected of them. Teachers felt that children's spelling needs were being efficiently addressed. Regular test results showed which children were needing more assistance with spelling. Parents knew how spelling was being taught in school.

The major deficiencies in such an approach included the evidence that children might memorise words from lists but often not spell them correctly when they used them later in their writing (lack of *generalisation* and *transfer* of learning). There was also a major problem created by providing a common spelling list for all students in the class, when clearly there was wide variation in the children's spelling ability and achievement levels. Some teachers responded to this difference in ability by presenting more than one list, each at a different level of difficulty but this was not common practice. The most serious limitation in the list approach was that teachers often expected children to memorise the words without having taught them any specific strategies to use when attempting to learn words. The expectation was that rote learning through repetition and practice would establish storage of specific word patterns in each child's long-term memory. For some students such an approach was simply not successful.

Over a period of time, this formal approach to spelling instruction fell into disrepute, mainly for the reasons given above, but also because beliefs about children's acquisition of literacy were changing rapidly. During the late 1970s and the 1980s significant shifts occurred in the general approach to literacy teaching in primary schools. There was a movement away from skills-based instruction to a more holistic and integrated approach to reading, writing and spelling.

In recent years, the development of children's literacy skills has been facilitated in primary schools through what is termed the 'whole language' approach to listening, speaking, reading and writing (Cambourne 1988; Goodman 1986). In this approach, spelling is usually dealt with almost entirely within the context of the children's daily writing, rather than as an area of skill deserving instructional time and effort in its own right. Teaching spelling as a separate subject is frowned upon, since it is felt that such an approach 'decontextualises' word study and does not link the importance of spelling with authentic attempts at communication. It is believed that studying words in isolation will not help the child to transfer and use this knowledge when writing.

In the whole language approach, the underlying belief is that children can be helped to acquire proficiency in spelling simply through engaging in a great deal of daily writing with regular constructive feedback from the teacher and from peers. Assistance in developing spelling skill is mainly directed toward each individual student, based on his or her immediate needs during a writing task. Little time (if any) is devoted to whole-class spelling or word-study lessons. The approach is deemed to be a 'natural' way for children to acquire the knowledge and skills needed for spelling, and is therefore seen as being preferable to any form of direct teaching based upon some pre-determined spelling list or programme.

In theory, the whole language approach to spelling appears to be an excellent way to individualise instruction; but in practice it is an extremely difficult approach to implement. In classrooms containing twenty-five or more students, it is virtually impossible to find the necessary time to devote to each individual student as he or she writes. Even if a few moments can be given to those individuals with the greatest need of assistance during a writing lesson, the

depth of teaching that can occur is inevitably very superficial and may have no lasting benefit for the child. It can also be argued that dealing only with individual words as they occur at random in a child's writing represents a *fragmented* approach to spelling instruction. An essential part of understanding how words are constructed involves recognising that many words share common and predictable letter sequences. Studying word families and discussing their similarities and differences has always been an important activity in this respect. It does not make sense to leave children to acquire this vital knowledge through incidental learning from individual words taught in isolation.

Increasing concern is being expressed about the suitability of whole language 'immersion' methods for children with learning difficulties. Graham and Harris (1994) have remarked that attempting to learn to spell primarily through incidental learning is a highly questionable approach for students with special educational needs. They state:

> We believe that these whole language methods of learning to spell are not powerful enough for students who are at risk or who have learning problems … (and) … in our opinion, advocates of incidental learning in spelling are overly optimistic. (p. 283)

This view is supported by Mather and Roberts (1995) who suggest that students with spelling difficulties do not learn effectively through holistic approaches to literacy. They do not develop an understanding of spelling generalisations simply through random experience with words. Similarly, Fulk and Stormont-Spurgin

(1995) have expressed grave doubts that students with learning disabilities will 'spontaneously' acquire spelling skills merely from exposure to literature-based programs and an encouragement to invent the spelling of any word they wish to write.

Have we lost our way?

Under the influence of the whole language approach many teachers have become much less certain about how best to approach the teaching of spelling in their classrooms (Barone 1992). They feel that they should be doing more to foster spelling ability in their children, but they remain confused about the best way of achieving this end. As Peters and Smith (1993) have remarked:

> Whilst teachers recognise the importance of the freedom to compose without the constraints of 'getting it right' at the first attempt, they continue to be anxious about meeting the pressures for good spelling which come from outside the classroom. (p. vii)

A leading advocate for whole language, Mem Fox (1997) has queried:

> Why have some teachers stopped teaching things like spelling? I think they heard statements such as: "You don't do spelling lists in whole language", so they stopped teaching spelling altogether. It was the wrong message. We must teach spelling. We need the power of being able to spell correctly. (p. 124)

In response to their own concerns, some teachers have resorted again to the use of weekly spelling lists and tests. Others make use of published spelling programmes and word-building games, exercises or puzzles. Unfortunately, many of the teachers using these approaches are not sure how to embed them effectively within the context of a total literacy programme. The lists, programmes and games are often used in isolation, almost as ends in themselves, without reference to context. In this situation the criticism that the content of the programme does not generalise to children's everyday writing is valid.

Some teachers also appear not to realise that the main aim in engaging in word study activities with children is to help them to acquire useful strategies (plans of action) for learning to spell or check any words they may need to use (Fulk 1997; Wong 1986). While there is some merit in learning the individual words in a particular list, the real value comes from *learning how to learn words*. For example, children should be helped, through explicit teaching, to decide whether a particular word in a list is most easily mastered by attending to the syllables and sounds within it (the phonemic or phonetic strategy), by remembering its visual appearance (the visual imagery strategy), by utilising information about the units of meaning that have been combined to produce the word (the morphemic strategy), by comparing the new word with one that is already known (the strategy of spelling by analogy), or by using some combination of these and other strategies.

Strategies for spelling and checking words will be discussed fully in later chapters. The point to be made here is that often teachers are unaware of the need to adopt a strategic approach to spelling, but rather focus the children's attention merely on rote memorisation of the words in a list. Read and Hodges (1982) have rightly observed that:

> learning to spell is not simply a matter of memorizing words but in large measure a consequence of *developing cognitive strategies* for dealing with English orthography [emphasis added]. (p. 1762)

Spelling is a *thinking process*, not a rote learning task. The development of spelling ability involves a process of learning to apply different strategies appropriately.

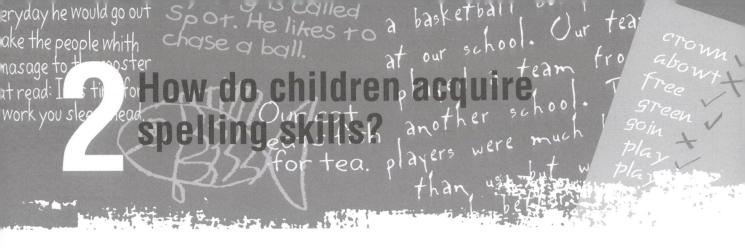

2 How do children acquire spelling skills?

According to most experts in this field (eg. Bissex 1980; Gentry 1981; Gentry & Gillet 1993; Moats 1995; Zutell 1998), learning to spell is a *developmental* process. Studies have indicated that spelling ability develops through a series of stages, each stage reflecting the children's current knowledge about speech sounds (phonemes), the relationship of these sounds to letters and letter-strings (grapho-phonic knowledge), and the units of meaning within words (morphemes). The stages also reflect the extent to which children have acquired specific strategies for visualising, writing and checking words.

Developmental stages in spelling acquisition

The key features of the developmental stages are presented below. It must be noted that, although age levels for typical acquisition have been suggested for each stage, these are only at best very rough approximations. A few children will pass through each stage earlier than the ages suggested here; and students with learning difficulties will be very much later in attaining mastery of the knowledge, skills and strategies typical of each stage. A few students may even leave school without having reached the final stage of independence in spelling, and may continue to have difficulties with spelling throughout their lives.

It is also important to point out that a child's rate of progress through the stages is influenced by the instruction he or she has received (Tangel & Blachman 1995). Some children with a natural aptitude for spelling will progress quite rapidly, with little or no explicit teaching. Others will make much greater progress if explicitly taught the knowledge, skills and strategies needed to take them from one stage to the next.

Stage 1: Pre-phonemic

Typical period of development: 3+ years to 5+ years.

'Pretend writing'. The child imitates writing by copying down or inventing random strings of letters. Capital letters are used much more frequently than lower case letters. The letters have no relationship to sounds within words.

Stage 2: Early phonetic

Typical period of development: 4+ years to 6+ years.

The child begins to use incidentally acquired knowledge of letter names and sounds in an attempt to write words (e.g. *yl = while*; *lefnt = elephant*; *erpln = aeroplane*; *rsk = ask*). Consonants are used much more consistently than vowels.

The creation of invented spellings by young children is considered to be an indication that they have started to develop an awareness of the internal sound structure of spoken words and how these units can be represented in print (Ehri 1989; Tangel & Blachman 1995).

This example from the South Australian Spelling Test (see Appendix 3) shows that the child (age 9 years 11 months, with learning difficulties) is still unable to correctly identify the middle vowel sound in the words *van*, *jam*, and *sit*; and does not identify the final sound in *lost*. The child is, however, about to enter Stage 3, the phonetic stage.

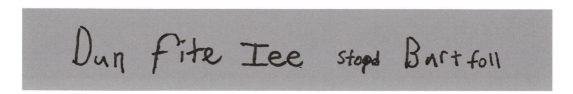

Stage 3: Phonetic

Typical period of development: 5+ years to 7 years.

While most researchers describe this as *the* phonetic stage, there are actually several different sub-stages within it.

In the beginning the child is making more accurate use of regular sound-symbol relationships. In doing so, most irregular words are written as if they are phonetically regular (e.g. *sed = said*; *becos = because*; *wos = was*).

The words below are fairly typical of children in the age range 6 years to 7 years attempting to spell *done*, *fight*, *eye*, *stopped* and *beautiful*.

Children at this stage will still attempt to spell difficult words, some of which result in good approximations, others less so. Consider the attempt of this girl in Year 2 at writing the sentence: *I saw a crocodile and in the crocodile was a ghost.*

I see a gruooo undin The gruooo Was a gos

She also wrote elsewhere in her story that the crocodile had *mean jaws*.

meen yoors

As children move through this stage they become better able to identify sounds within more complex words. In the intermediate stage they may still have difficulty in discriminating certain sounds accurately enough to match them with the appropriate letter or letter cluster. This difficulty is reflected in the words they write (e.g. *druck* = *truck*; *grive* = *drive*; *chrane* = *train*; *sboon* = *spoon*). They may also have difficulty in attending to all sounds within a word (e.g. *bow* = *blow*; *srong* = *strong*; *chrch* = *church*). Consider this child's attempt at writing the sentence: *I saw a tall wave [and] I ran to shore*:

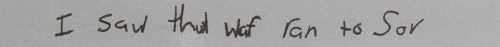

I saw thal waf ran to Sor

Towards the end of the phonetic stage a few common letter-strings and *morphographs* (the written equivalent of a morpheme) are remembered and reproduced easily and accurately as whole units (e.g. *un-*, *-ing*, *-ed*, *-s*). A few common vowel digraphs are also known (e.g. *-ee-*, *-oo-*).

It should be noted that the majority of students with poor spelling skills has reached this phonetic stage in their development but have not progressed beyond it. They need to be taught to use strategies such as visual imagery and spelling by analogy (see Chapter 4).

Stage 4: Transitional

Typical period of development: 6 years to 11+ years.

At this stage there is evidence that students have acquired a much more sophisticated understanding of word structure. They are becoming increasingly confident in using commonly occurring letter-strings such as *-ough*, *-ious*, *-ai-*, *-aw-* to represent sound units within words. They are also making reliable use of familiar words, or parts of words, when attempting the spelling of unfamiliar words (spelling by analogy).

In general, students at this stage are relying more on visual strategies rather than phonetic strategies alone to check the accuracy of what they have written. Also of help to them at this stage is their growing awareness of the way in which units of meaning (morphemes) are combined in complex words, sometimes with a particular rule needing to be applied (e.g. *un-happ-(y)i-ness*, *penalty - penalties*, but *monkey - monkeys*).

At this stage, most students who are progressing normally and engaging in a great deal of writing have stored a considerable mental 'bank' of correct word images. They can write almost all common words with a high degree of automaticity, and they have an increasing pool of known letter-sequences from which to draw when attempting to spell unfamiliar words. Students who engage in a great deal of reading are adding significantly to this bank of word images through increased exposure to print; and conversely, students who read very little are likely to be remaining at the phonetic stage when spelling.

Stage 5: Independence

Typical period of development: From 11+ years.

At this stage the student has almost perfect mastery of even the most complex grapho-phonic principles. Occasionally a word will still give the individual some difficulty; but he or she will have available for use a very wide range of strategies for checking and self-correcting words. Proof-reading skills are used by the student with increasing proficiency.

Students at the independence stage will still make some unusual errors and fail to detect them when proofreading their work. Note, for example, the two unusual spellings of went (wen't) and the spelling of told in the following material written by a boy aged 10 years:

We saw a Gorrila chasing two naked People, we calld out to. the Two People they ran Strait to us then a vampier came stait to us he wen't to suck my Blood, my friend hit him with a stick, It was very Sharp, he hit him in the heart all this blood wen't over me. me and my friends ran home we tolled our mums but they Just Said calm down son it will Be ok,?.

Using the developmental stages for diagnostic purposes

Examination of a child's unaided writing will often help a teacher determine the overall stage of development the child has reached (Westwood 1997). For example, a child whose work exhibits a high proportion of phonetic spellings will almost certainly benefit from being taught rather different word-attack strategies from a child whose errors indicate a lack of phonemic awareness. Similarly, a child who has no firm grasp of the correct spelling of certain suffixes and the rules that govern their attachment to words, will need explicit teaching and practice in this area.

It must be pointed out, however, that when an individual progresses beyond the beginning stage of spelling acquisition it is very common to find that his or her written work exhibits error-types typical of two or more different stages of development. This will occur, for example, when an older student is required to write about an unfamiliar topic with unique terminology. The student has had little or no prior exposure to these terms in print, and will almost certainly have to resort to a phonetic approach, spelling the words as they sound. Similar regressions can be seen in the writing of younger children, who may resort to early phonetic, or even pre-phonemic spelling, when very unfamiliar words are attempted (Moats 1995). For example, when children in primary school Years 4 and 5 were asked to spell the word *sufficient* their phonetic attempts included the following, shown here.

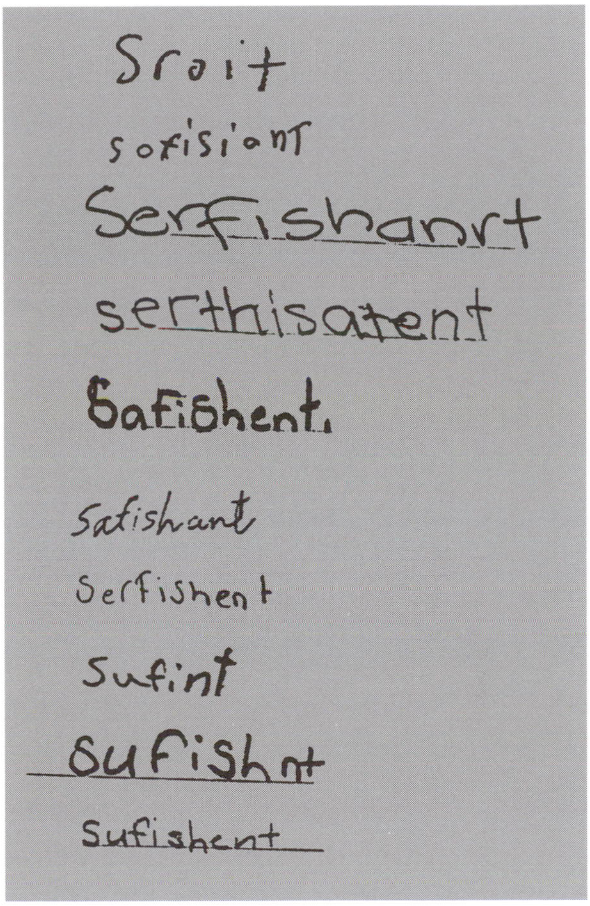

Sroit

sofisiont

Serfishanrt

serthisazent

bafishent.

safishant

serfishent

sufint

sufishnt

sufishent

When seeking to determine the overall stage of development a particular student has reached in spelling, it is always advisable to adopt the following approach:

- examine several different samples of unaided written work covering different subject matter and produced under different conditions (e.g. a short passage written from dictation; a story created by the student; notes taken from a lecture);

- discuss with the student the strategies he or she uses when faced with writing an unfamiliar word;

- observe the child as he or she writes, and again ask how the student attempted to spell the more difficult words.

Do we spell by mouth, ear, eye, hand, or brain?

The answer to the question above is that we almost certainly use all of these resources and modalities on the path to becoming proficient spellers (Westwood 1994). The relative importance of any one of these sources of information over any other tends to relate to the child's age and stage of development, and to the familiarity or complexity of the word being written.

Spelling by ear and mouth

Research has shown that in the early stages of learning to read and spell, it is important that a child can identify the different sound units within spoken words (phonemic awareness) (e.g. Ball & Blachman 1991; Goswami 1992). Studies have clearly demonstrated that the ability to work with the sounds of the language is crucial to the development of proficient spelling (Brann 1997). These phonological skills include the ability to recognise rhyme and pattern, to

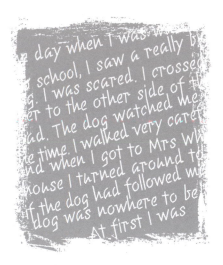

discriminate sameness and difference in words, to be able to analyse words into their component sounds and to synthesise or blend the sounds back into whole words again, and the ability to recall a correct sequence of sounds. As indicated above, children's early invented spelling reflects the way in which they are beginning to notice sounds within words and are attempting to represent these sounds with appropriate letters. At any age level, individuals will 'spell by ear' a word they have never seen in print. They will, however, tend to modify what they have written if the letter sequence does not 'look correct', given their prior experience of written English.

Obviously, simply identifying sounds in words provides a necessary but insufficient condition for spelling. The learner must also acquire a knowledge of which letters and letter clusters represent the sounds in print. As Pumfrey and Reason (1991) point out, that basic awareness of the sound-symbol relationship in English needs to be developed to a level of automaticity for fluent writing and spelling, as well as for reading.

It is fairly important that children can *say* clearly the words they wish to write. Working out the sounds they will need to use to spell the word usually requires them to articulate the word correctly. Inaccurate pronunciation can lead to errors. For example, 'our' written as 'are' is a common error made by primary age children ('this is are house'). Even in the case of older students with spelling difficulties, how a word is said often determines how the word will be written. If, for example, students say 'Feb-u-ary' it is unlikely that they will spell it as February. If they say 'somethink' for something, or 'samridge' for sandwich, that is how they are likely to spell those words. There are occasions, of course, when poor or careless speech articulation does not correlate highly with spelling ability; but speech is one possible factor to consider when searching for reasons for a particular student's problems. Hoffman (1990) points out that children with articulation or phonological problems sometimes misspell words containing the specific sound units with which they have most difficulty.

Spelling by eye

The most common way of checking one's own spelling and detecting errors is to look carefully at the written word and ask oneself, 'Does this word look right?' Writers will sometimes stop while writing simply because a word they have written doesn't 'look right' on the page, and they may decide to refer to a dictionary or to the spell-checker on the computer.

Proficient spellers appear to make very effective use of visual information when writing words. The increasing ability to recognise commonly occurring letter strings, and to store mentally a bank of high-frequency words known instantly by sight, are the two main characteristics of the 'transition stage' of spelling development. They represent significant steps in progress toward greater independence. Andrews and Scarratt (1996) have observed that skilled spelling reflects highly effective 'lexical storage' and retrieval processes in memory. 'Lexical storage' implies that the word image, or some key feature of its letter pattern, is stored in the learner's mental 'word bank' and is recognised instantly by sight and written correctly without conscious effort.

As a child moves out of the phonetic stage of spelling he or she begins to rely much more on the visual characteristics of a word, and very much less on a simplistic translation from sound to symbol. Moseley (1997) confirms that good spellers eventually come to rely on visual as much as phonological skills in spelling but he suggests that this may not occur much before the age of 11 years.

Read and Hodges (1982) state that part of becoming a good speller involves internalising the visual characteristics of words through extensive experience with written language. It is important to recognise that automatic recall of correct spelling patterns is one aspect of what psychologists call an individual's fund of 'declarative knowledge' (Gagne, Yekovich & Yekovich 1992). For example, through experience and teaching the individual *knows* that the word *house* is written using that sequence of letters. He or she also *knows* that the spelling *howse* does not look right because it does not match the image of the word stored in long-term visual memory.

In a later section particular attention will be given to the teaching of strategies that will help students to make more effective use of visual perception and visual imagery when spelling.

Spelling by hand

Since the spelling of a word is typically produced by the physical action of writing, it is fair to assume that kinaesthetic memory may also be involved in the storage and retrieval of spelling patterns, particularly those of very high frequency words. The extremely rapid speed and high degree of automaticity with which a competent speller translates a familiar word from its meaning to its graphic representation supports the view that kinaesthetic (motor) memory is involved, at least to some extent. Peters (1974a) regards accurate spelling as being quite heavily dependent upon 'motor habits'. The frequent action of writing may be one of the ways of establishing the stock of images of commonly occurring words and letter-strings in orthographic memory. According to Nichols (1985):

> Spelling is remembered best in your hand. It is the memory of your fingers moving the pencil to make a word that makes for accurate spelling. (p. 3)

Some researchers (e.g. Cripps 1990; Peters 1985) have observed a connection between swift, neat handwriting and spelling ability. It cannot be inferred that good handwriting *per se* causes good spelling; but laboured handwriting and uncertain letter formation almost certainly inhibit the easy development of automaticity in spelling. There have been suggestions that spelling development is aided by learning joined handwriting from the beginning of school entry, rather than first learning to print each separate letter (Cripps 1990). Moseley (1997) queries this practice, indicating that there is little evidence that learning joined writing helps beginning spellers to store commonly occurring letter-strings.

Spelling by brain

Some writers (e.g. Rowe & Lomas 1996) encourage teachers and students to regard spelling as a thinking and problem-solving activity. Working out the most probable way to spell an unfamiliar word requires the child to compare and contrast the word mentally with a known word. Arriving at a good approximation of a spelling may be facilitated if the child can deduce the morphemes involved in that particular word. For example, if a student has written a book in class he or she may want a friend to write a *Foreword* to the text. There is a temptation to write *Forward*, but thinking about the meaning of the term leads the student to realise that the first part of the word implies 'coming before' or 'in front of' (*fore* rather than *for*); and that *word* fits the context here, rather than *ward*. According to Elbro and Arnbak (1996), a knowledge of morphology can help with spelling. The most economical and efficient way to store spelling patterns in the long-term memory may well be by their morphemes rather than as whole word forms. English spelling appears to be much more logical when we understand that words are made up from meaningful units (morphemes) (Weckert 1989).

The ability to recall and apply spelling rules, or to recognise when a word is an exception to a rule, also reflects a rational and thoughtful approach to spelling. Similarly, devising some form of mnemonic to help one store and recall a particularly difficult word illustrates a creative solution to that particular problem. Another example of reasoning applied to spelling involves making a decision about the best strategy to use to learn or check a difficult word. Students should be able to look at a group of relevant thematic words and decide how best to go about the task of learning and remembering them.

The brain allows the learner to coordinate and integrate the various sources of cognitive and perceptual information that are available to help with the spelling of words. As the learner progresses through the various stages from novice to proficient speller, he or she gains greater control of these sources of information, and can use each to its best advantage. 'Connectionist' models of proficient spelling argue a close interaction between phonological, visual, semantic, kinaesthetic and morphological knowledge (Moats 1995; Leary & Johncock 1995). These models also suggest that the more frequently words and letter-strings are seen and written, the more powerful they become and the more likely they are to be recalled and used appropriately.

A model of the spelling process

The notion of a 'dual coding system' for processing and storing a variety of verbal and visual information has been suggested by Clark and Paivio (1991). In the field of spelling a dual coding system seems to be particularly relevant. A simplified model of the spelling process can illustrate how one of two different pathways may be followed according to the writer's familiarity with a particular word (see Fig. 1).

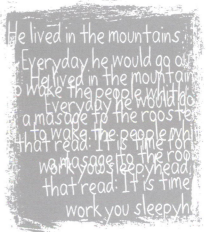

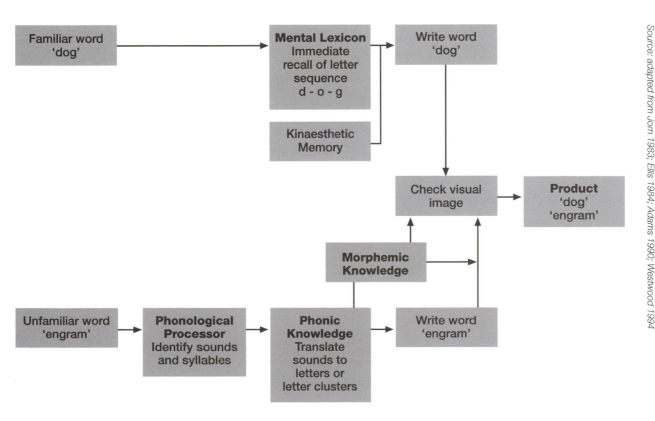

Source: adapted from Jorn 1983; Ellis 1984; Adams 1990; Westwood 1994

Figure 1: Theoretical model of the spelling process

The dual-processing model suggests that information about the *sound structure* of words is stored in a mental 'phonological information bank', while *visual information* about words and letter-strings is stored separately. Very familiar words appear to be retained efficiently in the writer's long-term visual and semantic memory store (or mental lexicon). This is referred to by some researchers as the 'visual-orthographic' memory bank (Moats 1995). This store is accessed easily for instant retrieval of information about whole words and common letter-strings. Familiar words retrieved from this store can be written with a high degree of automaticity. To some extent, motor memory of the writing or typing of the particular letter sequence may also support this process. On the other hand, unfamiliar words have to be processed quite differently by giving attention to the component sounds within the word, and the mapping of these sound units to probable letter sequences. This process to some extent may be supported by morphological knowledge of the specific meaning of parts of words.

Proficient spellers draw easily and appropriately on both banks of knowledge as they write. The most commonly written words require no mental effort for their retrieval. More conscious effort has to be devoted to writing complex and less frequently used words. In both cases, however, the writer appears to process the word visually as it is written to check that it 'looks right'.

The link between reading and spelling

Spelling ability was once considered merely to be a by-product of reading experience. It was thought that as children steadily built a stock of words known instantly by sight, and as they acquired phonic decoding skills for reading, they would simultaneously be able to write and spell words. This has been shown not to be the case. As Read and Hodges (1982) point out, spelling and reading are not simply the same process employed in reverse, and they remind us that not all good readers are good spellers.

Bradley (1983) suggests that reading, as a cognitive process, is generally easier than spelling. In reading, one can use contextual information to aid word recognition. Spelling differs from reading in that it requires accurate retrieval and reproduction of sequences of letters which cannot be guessed from context (semantic cues) or from sentence structure (syntactical cues) (Reason & Boote 1994; Peters 1974b). It is probable that the links between spelling skills and reading are strongest when the learner is attempting to decode an isolated word with no supporting context (Zutell 1998). In this case attention has to be given to translating letter patterns to sound.

While reading and spelling skills do interrelate, they tend to function independently of one another, particularly in the early years of learning (Clarke-Klein 1994). For example, some of the work of Bryant and Bradley (e.g. 1980) indicates that 6-year-old children appear to approach the processes of reading and spelling quite differently. When reading, they tend to use visual and contextual information; but for spelling they use phonological information. For most learners, increasing experience with print and writing diminishes this difference over time; and as children become more proficient with reading and writing, they make more effective and integrated use of visual, phonological and contextual information. By the age of 8 years the correlation between spelling ability and reading achievement is in the order of .89 to .92, suggesting a very close (but not perfect) association between the two processes (Westwood 1973). The correlation never becomes perfect. Even as adults, most of us can quite easily read words that we possibly cannot spell correctly.

Although children do not learn to spell simply by engaging in reading (Peters 1985; Dougherty & Clayton 1998), most children do spontaneously begin to notice and store the most frequently occurring words and letter-strings the more they read. Moats (1995) suggests that they will be helped to do this most rapidly and successfully when letter sequences are pointed out to them and discussed; and when they engage in activities requiring this information to be recalled and used when writing. Researchers concerned with spelling development suggest that children, in addition to *informally* learning how to spell through reading and writing, need to explore English spelling by investigating quite deliberately how words are constructed (Barone 1992; Templeton 1992; Fox 1997). According to Bouffler (1997), learning to spell involves the integration of a considerable amount of knowledge (phonemic, grapho-phonic, morphemic, semantic and syntactic) gleaned from all aspects of language, both written and oral. It is unrealistic to assume that all learners will acquire this important knowledge base incidentally, simply by engaging in reading activities.

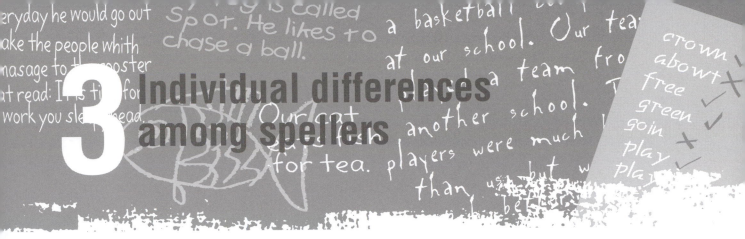

3 Individual differences among spellers

Learners appear to fall into one of three categories in relation to acquisition of spelling ability (Westwood 1979). The first category comprises those who seem almost to have a natural aptitude for language and easily accomplish the task of learning to spell in the same effortless way that they learned to speak, listen and read. It is difficult to place a figure on the percentage of students falling into this category, but unfortunately it is not large. The second, much larger group comprises those students who have no major problems in getting under way with spelling, but who benefit considerably from some degree of regular explicit teaching of word-study strategies appropriate to their level of development. Given this guidance, their progress through the various stages from beginner to independence is more likely to be smooth. The last group comprises those students who appear to find the task of spelling incredibly difficult, and who become frustrated by their inability to write correctly the words they can so easily use in speech. Students in this group are not necessarily of low intelligence; a few may be highly intelligent. Educational psychologists might label some of these students as 'learning disabled' or 'dyslexic'. They only know as much of the process of spelling as they have been directly taught. As Graham, Harris and Loynachan (1996) indicate, these students require much more extensive, structured and explicit teaching than is necessary for their peers.

Good spellers

Apart from their obvious accuracy and confidence when spelling words, what are the typical characteristics of 'good' spellers? It is important to ask this question, as the answers may help to indicate what less proficient spellers need to be taught.

Good spellers appear to have developed strategies for recognising sound sequences in words, grapho-phonic relationships, and visual patterns. They use phonetic, visual and morphemic information to help them write the words they want to use. They also have a good knowledge of word meanings. Good spellers also develop an attitude of self-monitoring; they take responsibility for their own learning and they check for errors (Leary & Johncock 1995).

According to Butyniec-Thomas and Woloshyn (1997), competent spellers possess a repertoire of effective spelling strategies, such as visual imagery and analogy, and can apply them appropriately. Moats (1995) agrees and suggests that:

> Good spellers are those who have learned to attend to several levels of word structure — sounds, syllables, and meaningful parts — as well as orthographic conventions for representing them. (p. 48)

Guidelines for teachers issued by The Department for Education and Children's Services (1997) in South Australia suggest that in addition to the points above, proficient spellers also develop a range of mnemonic strategies (memory joggers) to apply when learning particularly difficult and irregular words. They are also skilled in using appropriate resources to check the spelling of specific words (e.g. dictionaries, wall charts, vocabulary lists, computer spell-checkers).

From an early age good spellers may show a genuine interest in, and curiosity about, words. They ask what specific words mean when they hear them and when they encounter them in books or in the wider print environment. When they write they are willing to take risks, and rather than use a simple word in place of a more complex word, they will attempt the more difficult one and check it later.

It must be pointed out that proficient spellers are not always careful spellers; sometimes their ideas and the speed with which they want to record them take priority over accuracy. Good spellers still need to be taught effective strategies for proofreading their own work (see Chapter 4).

Average spellers

The majority of the population falls within this category. For most purposes of communication individuals in this group produce accurate spelling. They have progressed steadily through the stages of spelling acquisition, although they may still exhibit characteristics of an earlier stage when writing very unfamiliar words. They have a significant bank of words they can recall and spell correctly from memory; and most importantly, they tend to know when they need to check the spelling of a word they have just written.

Average spellers may have a somewhat more restricted range of spelling strategies to call upon when compared with very good spellers. The support required by the average speller often needs to focus on increasing the individual's repertoire of strategies for learning and recalling words, and on improving proofreading skills. Sometimes it is necessary to help students identify, and then remedy, any specific and persistent errors that occur within their written work.

Poor spellers

The weaknesses evident in the spelling of students with learning difficulties and learning disabilities may be related to underlying problems with language, memory, phonological awareness, visual processing and inefficient learning strategies (Fulk & Stormont-Spurgin 1995). On the other hand, poor spelling skills may be indicative of inadequate or insufficient instruction. In a few cases, the problems may be due to a combination of these two factors, with a student's underlying cognitive processing difficulties being exacerbated by teaching methods which take no account of them. For example, approaches to literacy instruction that do not explicitly teach phonological processing skills place some students at risk of failure. Methods that do not provide for adequate practice and overlearning in spelling also disadvantage some students. Within the context of whole language classrooms, Bean (1998) reminds teachers that they need to provide abundant opportunities for writing with feedback to occur to ensure that children's spelling skills are being advanced. She advocates daily writing, with the amount of support and direction given to students being determined by careful assessment of each individual's special needs.

It was pointed out earlier that phonological awareness is an essential prerequisite for spelling (Cataldo & Ellis 1990; Dougherty & Clayton 1998). According to Clarke-Klein (1994), the act of spelling is to a large degree a phonological translation task. Many students with spelling difficulties show poorly developed phonological analysis skills (Rohl & Tunmer 1988; Goswami 1992; Clarke-Klein 1994). This is particularly true in the case of dyslexic students. Read and Hodges (1982) report several studies indicating that poor spellers, particularly those assessed as dyslexic, have problems in segmenting spoken words into separate units of sound. These students also appear  to be particularly insensitive to the connection between letter patterns and the sound units they represent in words (Bradley 1990); or put more directly, they have particular difficulty in learning basic phonic skills. Intervention for such students should aim to help establish the connection between sound units and letter-strings (e.g. *str-*, *pre-*, *-ent*). Studying families of words sharing common letter sequences is particularly useful for this purpose (Varnhagen, C., Varnhagen, S. & Das 1992; Peters 1985). Dyslexic children and others with spelling problems need to be taught to identify similar letter-strings within different words. According to Gunning (1995), instant recognition of these letter-strings also facilitates rapid progress in reading.

Accurate identification of the sounds at the ends of words appears to be particularly difficult for some dyslexic students. They are reported to have major problems with identifying endings such as *-ed*, *-ent*, *-er*, *-ly*, *-ally*, *-ous*, *-ent* (Moats 1995). Persistent failure to spell word-endings (suffixes) also suggests a lack of morphemic knowledge. Elbro and Arnbak (1996) quote research indicating that young adults who are very poor spellers also tend to have poor awareness of morphemic principles. Dixon (1991) suggests that too little instruction is given in both phonemic and morphemic aspects of word study, compared with the attention given to purely visual memory approaches to spelling. Learning is much more likely to generalise to other words when phonemic and morphemic information is combined with visual information.

Some writers have suggested that the spelling errors made by dyslexic students are qualitatively different from those made by other students with learning difficulties. The errors they make are often referred to as 'bizarre' in that there is little connection between the letters they write and the sound units within the word (Thomson 1995). Others have argued that the dyslexic student's errors are simply typical of an earlier stage on the developmental spelling continuum, in this case the prephonemic stage (Padget, Knight & Sawyer 1996). Similarly, Mather and Roberts (1995) suggest that the onset of spelling difficulty in any individual is indicative of arrested progress through one of the stages in spelling development. If this is the case, then instruction for the individual needs to be linked carefully with that particular developmental stage (Gentry in Jongsma 1990) (see also Chapter 4). Problems will be exacerbated if a child is required to attempt to learn strategies beyond his or her current stage of development. As Ralston and Robinson (1997) indicate, the most effective spelling intervention for a student is one that takes into account the individual's current knowledge, skills, strategies and metacognitive processes.

When training in phonemic awareness is provided, spelling skills generally improve, at least toward a higher level within the phonetic stage of development. Studies have tended to show that where students with literacy problems improve over time they are beginning to make better use of phonological strategies for both reading and spelling (Ball & Blachman 1991; Waring, Prior, Sanson & Smart 1996).

Problems with phonological analysis, and with the use of grapho-phonic information, are not the only causes of spelling difficulty. These problems apply most to young students and to older students with dyslexia. A significant number of students with general learning difficulties have progressed to the phonetic stage of spelling, but then appear to remain there, unable to switch easily to the application of visual imagery and other strategies which would enable them to move to the next stage. Some poor spellers seem unable to conjure up a word image from their visual-orthographic memory, so they remain overly dependent on sound and spelling 'by ear' (Moats 1995).

The poorest performers seem to have a very restricted range of strategies to use when spelling, and their foremost need is to be taught other ways of writing and checking words. For such students, simply dealing incidentally with spelling as a minor aspect of writing activity is not enough. They need direct teaching of a wide range of effective strategies (Gentry & Gillet 1993; Ralston & Robinson 1997). Moats (1995) cites research to indicate that children do benefit from explicit teaching of word study and spelling strategies.

There is wide agreement that instruction in spelling for students with learning difficulties, while linked closely with writing for authentic purposes, needs also to be intense, direct, systematic and regular (Mather & Roberts 1995; Graham & Harris 1994). It must also be instruction that promotes full knowledge of the spelling system and how it operates.

A final word from Gentry (in Jongsma 1990):

> A spelling program must be based on current research and that research overwhelmingly rejects the notion that spelling is learned incidentally. (p. 60)

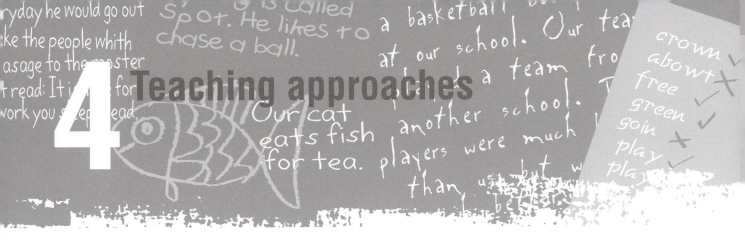

General principles

Redfern (1993) has suggested some basic principles to guide any approach to spelling instruction in the classroom. They include:

- building in children positive attitudes toward spelling;
- promoting their on-going interest in words and language;
- teaching strategies for learning to spell and check words.

Graham *et al.* (1996) also stress the vital importance of teaching children *strategies* for spelling, but indicate that an effective spelling programme must also involve three other components:

- frequent reading and writing;
- the direct teaching of high-frequency words;
- active involvement in comparing and contrasting words according to patterns and structures (word study).

Some of these basic principles will be discussed in more detail in this section.

Attitude and interest

The teacher has an essential role to play in raising children's interest in words and in influencing their attitude toward spelling. Attitudes are acquired almost entirely by observation of the behaviour and reactions of others and cannot be 'taught' directly (Gagne, Briggs & Wager 1992). If teachers are interested in, and enthusiastic about words, this enthusiasm is conveyed indirectly to children, and they are likely to become more interested themselves. There is a need, from the very start, to build a positive and supportive classroom environment where children are encouraged to take risks and experiment with their writing (Bean 1998). Teachers need to show genuine interest in children's attempts at spelling unfamiliar words, and descriptive feedback to children should be positive and helpful, not critical in a way that undermines confidence.

Word study

Studying words is an essential component of any effective classroom approach to spelling. As Templeton (1992) has observed:

Spelling knowledge grows out of and supports reading, writing and vocabulary study. *It also grows out of examining words in and of themselves.* [emphasis added] (p. 455)

The type of word study undertaken with any individual student or group of students should reflect an awareness of the stage of development they have reached. With beginning spellers the focus may be at the phonemic awareness stage, with the analysis of simple spoken words into sound patterns. For example, drawing the children's attention to the way in which we can 'stretch out' a word as we say it, and hear the sounds more clearly: *S - a - m; t - o - p; sh - o - p.* Games can be played to help young children develop the ability to identify what is termed the *onset* and *rime* characteristics of single syllable words *(onset* = the first sound unit heard in the word; *rime* = the vowel and all letters following it: e.g. *track*: /*tr*/ [onset] /- *ack*/ [rime]).

Activities to help children blend sounds to make words can also be used: 'I spy with my little eye a *cl - o - ck*. What can I see?' At this stage early spelling is being directly related to phonemic awareness training (Nicholson 1994). At the same time the children will need to be taught explicitly how to map the sounds they hear in words to particular letters and letter clusters. At first this will usually involve single letters, followed by commonly occurring digraphs (e.g. *sh, ch, th, ck*) and consonant blends (e.g. *bl, tr, cr, st, pr*). At this stage, some children will also begin to recognise and store certain phonemically-irregular but high-frequency words which they will need to remember and write without reference to sound cues (e.g. *the, all, are, one*) (see Appendix 2)

With spellers already operating successfully within the phonetic stage of development, attention needs to be devoted to analysing words with slightly more complex structures, and also to helping the students to attend more carefully to key visual features of particularly difficult words. In order to move from the phonetic stage to the transition stage students will need to make more effective use of visual imagery. Additional advice on improving visual strategies for spelling is provided below.

As they move from the phonetic to the transitional stage, spellers also need to make more effective use of knowledge of letter-strings representing more complex sound units within words (e.g. *-ight, -ous, -ough*). Coltheart and Leahy (1996) suggests that children need a great deal of experience with basic grapho-phonic decoding of unfamiliar words before they can easily use these larger units (letter-strings) for more rapid and automatic word recognition and spelling. Similarly, spelling by analogy becomes easier as the child gets older and more experienced with word forms and can better hold important letter-strings in mind (Redfern 1993). It is at this stage that attention also needs to be given to the mastery of some of the variations in vowel sounds. Children need to consider vowels used in combination with other letters (e.g. *-ar, -aw, -ie-, -ea-*). The section entitled 'Learning to manage the vowel system' in Rowe and Lomas (1996) is particularly helpful at this stage. Also of great value are the activities embedded in the Spelling Book provided as part of the Teaching Handwriting, Reading and Spelling Skills (THRASS) program (Davies and Ritchie 1996).

At the transition stage students need to be helped to make efficient use of the strategy of spelling by analogy. They need to discuss how knowledge of one word can help to predict the spelling of another word. Much of the content of spelling instruction will focus on recognition of commonly occurring letter-strings, including prefixes and suffixes. To assist with spelling at this stage students need to be taught basic morphemic principles (for example, how the word *try* becomes *tried* and *tries*; or how the word *study* becomes *studied*). Given that many teachers are themselves not particularly confident in dealing with this aspect of written language, reference to Dixon and Engelmann's (1976) *Morphographic Spelling* programme can be extremely helpful.

To aid word study Gaskins *et al.* (1997b) developed a programme in which students were instructed (through direct teaching and modelling) how to analyse and segment target words and how to match these sound units to letter-strings. Students were also taught to use words they already knew to decode and encode words that were unfamiliar. The authors stated that:

> We realized that word-learning efficiency could be improved by teaching students procedures for learning words in a fully analysed way, rather than expecting them to figure out the spelling system on their own. (p. 326)

Graham, Harris and Loynachan (1996) are in full agreement with this perspective and suggest that an important component in any effective spelling programme is helping students to learn how to recognise and take advantage of the regularities and patterns underlying English spelling.

As students become increasingly aware of spelling patterns and their applications they can better predict the structure of unknown words. When they become familiar with meaningful units such as prefixes and suffixes, as well as root words, their grasp of word structure expands (Dale, O'Rourke & Barbe 1986). Cunningham (1998) has recommended using lists of multisyllabic words, such as *impossible*, *impatient*, and *improper* to help students at the transitional stage of development identify and master common spelling patterns based on units if meaning or on phonic principles.

Zutell (1998) has suggested that when students operate with groups of letters rather than single letters, English spelling is more consistent than it at first appears when analysed in terms of *single* letter-to-sound correspondences. At the level of the individual letter, English orthography is highly variable, but this variability is reduced when children begin to process clusters of letters (Bradley 1983).

Studies indicate that sound units in words are represented predictably by specific letters or clusters of letters at least 80 per cent of the time. The English spelling system is then not as chaotic as many would claim (Bouffler 1997).

Allocating time for word study

There are many ways in which word analysis can be embedded within the total literacy programme. The most common approach is for the teacher to set aside a brief period of time on several occasions in each week to focus on interesting words from the children's own writing, and words that are related to some of the subjects and themes studied within the curriculum. These brief word study sessions are often referred to as 'mini lessons' (O'Flahavan & Blassberg 1992; Vaughn, Bos & Schumm 1997).

Fox (1997) described how she uses mini lessons and games to integrate word study activities within her programme. She causes children to focus on, and take interest in, the ways in which words are constructed from particular letter-strings, such as -ough or -tion, or, for example, how the consonant digraph ck is often used to end words but never to begin them. The content for her word study is taken from vocabulary used in the children's own reading and writing, not from predetermined lists. Her approach to embedding explicit spelling instruction within her whole language programme is fully supported by Bouffler (1997) who indicates that spelling instruction would never have been abandoned within whole language classrooms if teachers had really understood the philosophy behind the approach.

Other writers (e.g. Bartch 1992; Westwood 1994; McCoy 1995; Davies & Ritchie 1996) advocate a rather more formal allocation of time for specific instruction in phonics and spelling in the early primary school years, particularly for those students who are experiencing difficulties in learning. This specific time allocation does not replace, but rather complements, the attention given to spelling and word study within any writing lesson.

To do justice to programmes specifically designed to increase spelling skills, adequate time must be made available in the school day. Most of these programmes completely lose their impact and benefits if they are implemented piecemeal. Examples of such programmes include *Spelling Mastery* (Dixon & Engelmann 1990), *Morphographic Spelling* (Dixon & Engelmann 1976), *THRASS* (Davies & Ritchie 1996) (see Chapter 6). Where programmes of this type are used with whole classes, groups or individuals, it is essential that teachers do everything they can to ensure that the spelling principles studied within the programme are also used applied by the students when they write and edit their work. Teachers should anticipate the difficulty many students have in generalising important information studied in one context to another. Every opportunity must be taken to discuss with students how various principles and rules can be used in different writing contexts. Frequent review of these principles will also be a feature of an effective programme of instruction (Vaughn, Bos & Schumm 1997).

Strategy training

There can be no doubt that improvement in spelling can be achieved when students are taught more about *how* to learn words, and how to check the spelling of words they have attempted (Butyniec-Thomas & Woloshyn 1997; Fulk 1997). Effective instruction in spelling involves not only teaching knowledge about words (phonemic, grapho-phonic and morphemic), but also teaching specific *strategies* to enable students to approach the task of spelling an unfamiliar word, or checking the spelling of a word, with a systematic plan of action (Wong 1986; Snowball 1997a). Strategies are usually taught most effectively when the teacher models how he or she approaches the same task of spelling or checking a word. 'Thinking aloud' is the standard way of showing students how they might tackle the same problem. After demonstration, the students then need to have an opportunity to apply the strategy themselves with guidance and feedback from the teacher. Such strategies usually involve teaching the student to ask himself or herself a series of questions. For example:

- Do I know this word?
- How many syllables can I hear?
- Do I know any other words that sound almost the same?
- How are those words written?
- Does this word I have written look right?
- I'll try it again.
- Does this look better?'

During the primary school years children can be taught simple 'self-talk' strategies to apply when making discoveries about words. One example is the use of the *Talk to Yourself Chart* (Gaskins *et al.* 1997a; 1997b). The chart teaches a six-step procedure for studying a target word:

- The word is …
- Stretch the word … I hear the sounds …
- I see … letters
- The spelling pattern is …
- The vowel says …
- Another word like … is …

In a study of students in Year 5 by Ralston and Robinson (1997) they identified nineteen possible strategies that spellers might use. They stated that spelling accuracy is enhanced when several strategies for generating and checking words are used simultaneously. A similar view is presented by Salend (1994) who suggests that skills and strategies are more powerful when used in combination. The study by Ralston and Robinson also indicated that the students most frequently used only the strategies which they had been specifically taught (mainly grapho-phonic and visual recall), but some had also devised other strategies of their own. The writers comment that if students were to be taught to use a greater variety of spelling strategies they might use them more effectively and selectively when they write. The general evidence from this study seems to suggest that teachers themselves are not well acquainted with a broad range of spelling strategies. This message has important implications for reviewing the content of language arts methodology programmes in teacher education courses.

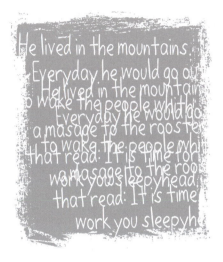

Among the specific strategies most commonly recommended is the use of visual imagery. This strategy needs to be taught to many children who appear not to be able to progress easily beyond the phonetic stage of spelling. The strategy is sometimes referred to as the 'whole word' method of learning to spell, implying that students will store the complete image of a particular word in memory. While this is a reasonable assumption to make if the word is short, the notion breaks down for longer words. The average 'visual attention span' of children in the primary grades does not allow for the processing and storage of other than very small words as 'wholes' (Harrison, Zollner & Magill 1996). The visual images that do need to be stored are the commonly occurring letter-strings that comprise most words.

Training visual imagery

Not all individuals appear to use visual imagery to the same degree when processing information. For example, some learners do not automatically create mental pictures as they read a novel. Some do not use visual imagery to 'picture in the mind's eye' the context of a word-problem in mathematics. Others do not support the recall of number facts by 'picturing' them as a number sentence (e.g. $3 + 7 = 10$) as well as trying to recall them auditorily. In general, the ability to use visual imagery is helpful to learning across a wide range of curriculum content. Training in visual imagery has been used successfully over many years to help students store and retrieve a variety of types of information (Hutton & Lescohier 1983; Bell 1991). The application of visual imagery training to enhance spelling ability has been well documented (e.g. Peters 1985; Sears & Johnson 1986; McLaughlin & Skinner 1996).

The 'look-cover-write-check' strategy, used in schools for many years, is based on improving the learner's visual memory for small words and letter-strings (McLaughlin & Skinner 1996). It is a strategy most appropriate for learning words that are phonemically irregular. The strategy is still effective for longer words, but it is likely that the learner actually performs two or more 'visual fixations' on the letter sequence, processing it not as a whole, but in convenient parts represented by specific letter clusters.

One version of the approach involves presenting a word on a card to the learner (e.g. *choir*). The learner is told:

- Use your eyes like a camera. Take a picture of this word *choir*.
- Close your eyes and imagine you can still see the word.
- Trace the letters in the air with your eyes closed.
- What colour are the letters in your mind?
- OK. Now imagine the letters have changed colour. What colour are they now?
- Open your eyes and write the word on your paper.
- Now check your spelling with the word on the card.

Peters and Cripps (1980) suggest getting the learners to pretend that they can see the word on the 'inside of their eyelids'.

Berninger *et al.* (1995) taught specific spelling strategies to students with spelling problems at the end of Year 3 as part of a general intervention to improve their writing skills. In particular, they taught a visual imagery strategy for spelling. The children were taught the following steps:

- Look at the word.
- Close your eyes and imagine you can see the word as you say it.
- Name the letters from left to right.
- Open your eyes and write the word.
- Check against the model.
- Repeat if necessary until the word can be recalled easily.

They also taught strategies for analysing words into syllables. The benefits of the training were still evident at a follow-up six months later.

Butyniec-Thomas and Woloshyn (1997) cite research studies that support the value of training children to create visual images of target words. In their study, Year 3 children undertook twenty minutes of strategy-training daily for one week. The imagery training involved teaching the students to close their eyes and imagine they were typing the word or painting the word on a screen or chalkboard. The strategy was modelled, its value discussed, practice was given, and daily review provided. They compared three groups: one received explicit strategy training alone (words not in context); one received explicit strategy training using words from whole language contexts; and the third group engaged in whole language writing activities without strategy training. The 'strategy training plus whole language' group produced the superior spelling results. The least effective approach was the whole language with no explicit instruction. These researchers concluded that:

> The provision of relevant writing experiences improved the spelling performance of some students, but most of the students required the support of formal spelling instruction in order to become proficient spellers. (p. 300)

In order to make maximum use of visual strategies for spelling it is essential that the students are encouraged to look at the target word with deliberate intent to hold the visual image (Redfern 1993). Further advice:

- Tell the learner to look carefully at the word and to think of other words with the same letter pattern.
- Make sure that the learner writes the word from memory, not from rote copying.

Repeated writing

It was once traditional practice to require students to write the corrected version of words ten times. In recent years this procedure has been used much less often because teachers feel that it does not result in effective learning. Redfern (1993) states categorically that copying out spelling corrections is of no value. This view needs to be challenged. Under the following conditions repeated writing of a correct word form can be helpful in facilitating its storage in long-term memory:

- The writer must want to master the spelling of that word.
- Full attention must be given to the writing task.
- Only a few words (no more than three) are treated this way in any one session.

Peters (1974a) sees spelling skill partly as a 'motor habit'. The frequent writing of a word with the letters in the correct sequence probably helps the learner to establish a motor pattern for that word in kinaesthetic memory. In much the same way, touch typing on a keyboard helps to establish automatic motor responses linked to high frequency words.

Interestingly, Redfern (1993), who says there is no value in repeated writing of words, also remarks elsewhere that teachers should not let uncorrected work go on indefinitely because 'bad habits get into the hand'. Grainger (1997) suggests that if young children spend too long practising incorrect spelling patterns through the use of invented spelling without corrective feedback, this can create on-going problems for some individuals. They are storing incorrect visual images of the words as well as the incorrect motor responses.

Simultaneous oral spelling (SOS)

This strategy was first developed by Gillingham and Stillman in 1960 and has been found useful in individual remedial tuition by Bryant and Bradley (1985). It is applicable across a wide age range, including secondary and tertiary education settings, as the use of the letter name rather than the sound, does not embarrass the older learner. If a student appears to have difficulty in holding visual images in memory, saying the letter names may help (Redfern 1993).

The steps in the SOS strategy are as follows:

- Select the word you wish to learn.
- Look at it carefully.
- Ask the instructor to pronounce the word clearly.
- Pronounce the word yourself.
- Say each syllable (in a polysyllabic word).
- Name the letters in sequence, and then say the word e.g. *w-o-r-l-d* = *world*.
- Repeat the letter naming step again.
- Write the word, naming each letter as it is written.
- Check and say the word.
- Write the word again from memory.

Old Way – New Way

This corrective strategy devised by Lyndon (1989) is designed to help a student overcome a persistent spelling error. Moats (1995) has observed, when children write a word the wrong way repeatedly before learning it correctly, the incorrect response is hard to remove and the correct habit difficult to establish.

When an incorrect visual spelling pattern or motor response has been internalised and stored by a learner it is very difficult to replace it with the correct response due to the power of what is termed 'proactive inhibition' or 'proactive interference'. What the learner already knows interferes with the re-learning process.

Lyndon's approach uses the student's error as the starting point for intervention. A memory of the incorrect (old) way of spelling the word is used to activate later an awareness of the new (correct) way of spelling the word. The following steps and procedures are used in Old Way – New Way:

- The student writes the word in the incorrect form.
- The student and teacher agree to call this the 'old way'.
- Alongside the incorrect spelling the teacher writes the new (correct) form.
- Teacher and student discuss the differences between the old and new forms, e.g. *thay* and *they*. The student says 'I used to spell it with an *a*, now I spell it with an *e. They*.' The *a* can be crossed out and the *e* underlined.
- Student writes the word again the old way.

- Student writes the word the new way and verbalises the difference.
- Five such repetitions of old way and new way are completed, with a verbal statement of the difference (I used to write it with an *a*, now I write it with an *e. They*).
- The word is now written six times in the new way using different size letters or different colour chalk or pen.
- The word is revised after a week, and again after another week.

Lyndon's strategy has much in common with other approaches where error imitation is used as a teaching point. Error imitation, followed by modelling of correct spelling, has been used in several controlled studies (e.g. Gerber 1986; Gordon *et al.* 1993). The teacher reproduces the student's error while the student watches. The teacher then writes the word correctly and together they discuss differences between the two words. The student then writes the word correctly several times from recall. Using this approach, students with learning disability improved significantly and were able to generalise spelling features from one list of words to another.

General-purpose strategy

Graham and Freeman (1985) and Fulk (1996) have used the following five-step strategy very successfully with learning disabled students. It has wide applicability, including use with adults. The strategy is particularly helpful when attempting to learn a word that does not conform to phonemic or morphemic principles (for example, a word imported from a foreign language).

Having selected a target word for study:
- Say the word.
- Write and say the word.
- Check the spelling.
- Trace and say the word.
- Write the word from memory and check it.

Instructional activities

Directed Spelling Thinking Activity (DSTA)

This activity is advocated by Graham, Harris and Loynachan (1996) for use with learning disabled students. The actual principles behind it merit wider application to all students who are still acquiring knowledge about the spelling system. DSTA is basically a word-study procedure in which a group of students are helped to compare, contrast and categorise two or more words based on points of similarity or difference. The aim of the activity is to raise the students' awareness of spelling patterns and grapho-phonic principles. For example, the students may explore words containing the long *a* sound, as in *pail, male* and *pay*. They discover that the same sound can be represented by different letter clusters. The students are then given lists of words, (or they search for words themselves), to classify into a similar category. Follow-up activities might include looking for words containing a target sound, or a specific sequence of letters, within their reading material. Over a period of time a class list of words that follow a particular rule, or are exceptions to that rule, is constructed and used regularly for revision.

Word Sorts

An activity very similar to Directed Spelling Thinking Activity is called Word Sorts. The students are provided with words on cards to be studied and compared. For example at a fairly simple level: *back, sock, black, suck, pluck, truck, lock, rack, kick, track, trick, block, brick, lick, rock, sack,* and *pack.* They are asked, 'What is the same about these words?' The response might be that they all end in *ck.* The words can, however, be categorised in other ways. The students are helped to sort the word cards into categories using longer letter-strings. At higher levels the students might be working with *-ation* words, for example, presentation, invitation, station, and relation. They might be studying the way in which vowels sounds are frequently modified by the consonant which follows them. In relation to this type of activity, Invernizzi, Abouzeid and Gill (1994) comment:

> Students must have the opportunity to examine, manipulate, and make decisions about words according to categories of similarities and differences. It is up to teachers to direct students' attention to a particular contrast and to create tasks that require students to do so. (p. 166)

The use of Word Sorts is strongly supported by Zutell (1998) as a valuable means of helping children recognise important letter patterns in and across words. Zutell states that middle primary school students introduced to Word Sorts showed positive changes in their spelling strategies, were enthusiastic about engaging in the activity, and indicated improved ability to use information about letter patterns to edit their own writing. Selection of the actual words for study must be made relative to the students' developmental spelling stage. For students with learning difficulties it is important to begin with easy, straightforward Word Sorts in which the students can quickly experience high levels of success. The cognitive demands of the activity can be increased slowly over time.

Word families

This is perhaps the most traditional way of helping children recognise the similarities among words. A word family could be based on a number of different criteria. For example:

- a rhyming sound pattern represented by simple letter-to-sound correspondences (e.g. *man, van, pan, fan, can, ran, tan*);

- a sound pattern represented by a long vowel, rather than a short vowel unit (e.g. *bind, find, kind, mind, wind, hind*; or *fame, game, lame, name, same, tame, flame, frame*);
- a sound pattern based on a particular letter-string (e.g. *right, tight, might, light, fight, sight, flight, bright*);
- words containing the same letter-string but with less predictable pronunciation (e.g. *bomb, comb, tomb*);
- words containing silent letters (e.g. *scent, climb, knee, wrap, gnaw, debt*).

Snowball (1997c) recommends word families to help build the child's knowledge of base words and their associated prefixes, suffixes, derivatives, and compound words. For example: *play, plays, played, playing, playful, playfully, replay, replays, replayed, replaying, player, playtime, playground.*

The important principle to stress here is that word families are an essential part of helping children understand word structures, but they should always be linked with the children's reading and writing needs (Bean 1998). If this does not occur there is a danger that the 'families' become a 'spelling programme' in their own right, with little likelihood that using them will generalise to the children's writing. One way of preventing this is to use words from the children's writing as the starting point in order to generate a specific word family for study.

Prompt Spelling

This peer tutoring activity was described by Watkins and Hunter-Carsch (1995). It involves secondary school students working in pairs, a good speller (prompter) with a less proficient speller (promptee) for about twenty minutes. It could equally well be used by an adult working in a tutorial role with an individual student.

The promptee selects up to five words he or she wants to learn from errors made in a recent piece of writing. The errors are copied into the first of four columns on a worksheet. The prompter articulates the target word clearly, stressing component sounds and syllables if necessary. This is repeated twice. The promptee underlines in the first column any part of the word he or she thinks might be incorrect. The pair discuss this and if necessary, changes are made. In the second column the promptee writes the correction. This is checked and discussed with the prompter. Together they look back at the original error and discuss which letters were incorrect. They now attempt to link the correct spelling with any other related words (e.g. with similar letter cluster, or similar silent letter, or similar point of irregularity). The promptee then writes any related words in the third column. Time is spent in studying the corrected spelling and the words generated from it. The promptee then covers the first three columns, states the error to be avoided, then writes the word correctly in the fourth column. The prompter then checks this and gives feedback. The procedure is then repeated with the second target word. The corrections are reviewed and if necessary practised at frequent intervals during the next few weeks.

The notion of using individual tutoring for spelling improvement in secondary school students is also supported by Hewson (1990). She established a system where parent volunteers worked directly with poor spellers using the look-cover-write-check strategy. The parents had first been trained in the strategy and also in the teaching and interpersonal skills required of a tutor (e.g. giving praise; encouraging the student to 'have a go'; not being too critical; using positive reinforcement). The outcomes from a five-week programme were positive. Using parents and other adults for coaching in spelling, both inside and outside the classroom context, is recommended by Vaughn *et al.* (1997).

Spelling lists

It was remarked earlier that in some classrooms the use of spelling lists has become much less popular in recent years. Some teachers feel that the use of such lists may lead to a return to isolated word drills and rote memorisation, culminating in a weekly test. They believe that words studied in this way are soon forgotten. Not all teachers agree with this perspective, and some find value in using lists for specific purposes.

The use of word lists can be defended on many counts. For example, the use of high-frequency word lists is fully justified. Snowball (1997b) points out that the 100 most frequently used words make up about half the written English language. Learning to spell these words correctly is therefore a high priority for all students. Mastery of the most commonly occurring words is of particular importance for students with learning difficulties because these are indeed the words they use in their writing. If priority is given to learning this relatively small core of words the students will make fewer errors in their writing and will find the task less daunting. Mastering the list of high frequency words yields high returns for the student (Harris *et al.* 1996). One of the most recent word frequency lists, *The Spelling for Writing List*, is provided by Graham, Harris and Loynachan (1994) (see Appendix 2).

Bean (1998) recommends guiding students to build lists of words that will serve their own writing needs and which they can use as a point of reference when writing and proofreading. She indicates that such lists might cover words the students need to use regularly (see above) and lists of their own spelling 'demons'. Vaughn, Bos and Schumm (1997) suggest that lists might comprise words students ask for in their writing, words frequently misspelled in their writing, and words related to new themes or topics.

In order to carry out the word study described in several of the activities above (particularly word families) it is obvious that to have lists of words illustrating specific sound-to-spelling patterns or depicting particular morphemic principles, is of great value. Teachers would not want to have to recreate these unnecessarily.

Polloway and Patton (1997) remind teachers of the need to do everything possible to help students transfer knowledge and skills gained from lists to their everyday writing:

> Although learning words in isolation facilitates acquisition, maintenance and generalization are achieved only when students are encouraged to make regular use of the words they have learned. (p. 290)

Computers (word processors)

Undoubtedly, the arrival of the word processor in the classroom heralded a new opportunity for students with learning difficulties to enter the realm of writing and composing with renewed enjoyment and satisfaction. Students with learning difficulties can now gain confidence in creating, spell-checking, editing, erasing and publishing their own materials.

Minton (1992) indicates that computers can help students with learning disabilities because:

- The medium itself is motivating.
- It provides for practice and overlearning.
- It gives immediate feedback.
- The work level can be adjusted to student's learning rate.
- It is an active way of learning, fully involving the student.
- Using a computer can be a private way of study, avoiding the close scrutiny of peer group.

There is a need to ensure that students do not come to rely entirely on the use of the in-built spell-checker to produce accurate writing. They must still retain personal responsibility for making an honest attempt at typing in the correct sequence of letters when spelling the word. A sound approach to use is to encourage the student to print the first draft of the piece of writing without using the spell check. The student and a partner (or the student and the teacher) can then read the print-out and discuss the spelling, as well as the ideas in the story. The student can use a pencil to circle any words he or she thinks may be incorrect. The teacher will be able to observe which words the student can self-correct, which words cannot be corrected without assistance and even more importantly, which misspelt words are not detected by the student (Westwood 1997).

For students with severe spelling difficulties the spell-checker on most word processors is not of much assistance. As Mather and Roberts (1995) point out, one must be a fairly proficient speller to use a spell-checker effectively and independently. In order for most spell-checkers to generate a correct spelling they must be able to recognise the original misspelling entered by the typist. Some students still operating at the prephonetic or early phonetic stage may type in a letter-string so unusual that it is not recognised by the program. According to a study carried out by MacArthur *et al.* (1996), only approximately one-quarter of errors are recognised by the computer. This is partly due to the problem identified above, but also relates to the computer's inability to detect the incorrect use of a word which has the correct spelling (e.g. *there* in place of *their*; *how* instead of *who*).

Another difficulty arises for the student who is also a poor reader. He or she may have great difficulty in deciding which is the correct word from a list of suggested spellings generated by the computer. Students also need to be able to read and understand the instructions associated with the spell-checker when these appear on the screen.

Teaching proofreading for spelling errors

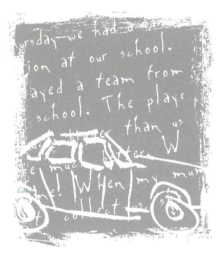

The process of proofreading written text is not easy. Even some adults find it extremely difficult to detect the errors that are present in their own work. The process requires the reader to move away from the powerful influence of the *meaning* of what is being read to allow careful attention to the actual letters and words on the page.

Bean (1998) and the Department for Education and Children's Services (SA) (1997) provide some useful advice to help children improve their skills in proofreading. The key ingredient is the teacher's demonstration of how to go about the process. Children need the teacher to model the following strategies, using the overhead projector, blackboard, or prepared sheets of text.

- Use a slip of paper or a ruler to cover all but the line you are checking.
- Experiment with starting at the bottom of the page and working upwards.
- Read slowly, word by word.
- Underline any word that needs to be checked.
- Write two or more versions of a word and try to decide which one looks correct.
- Sometimes exchange writing with a partner for proofreading purposes.
- Teach some of the typical symbols used by editors to signal changes needed in the text.

Wirtz *et al.* (1996) reported a small scale study in which third-year students were taught how to correct their own spelling errors from a dictated list using proofreading marks (such as 'wrong letter', 'letter missing'). The students then

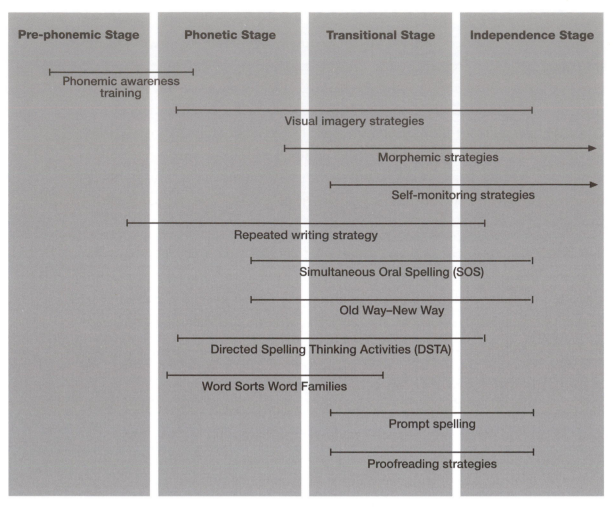

Figure 2: Guide to selecting stage-appropriate interventions

wrote the correct version of each word. They made better gains than students who simply copied the correction for each word several times and used the word in a sentence. These students also reported that they liked the method.

Matching intervention to stage of development

Figure 2 provides the teacher with some assistance in selecting spelling interventions that take account of the stage of development reached by a particular student or group of students. The chart is intended only as an approximate guide and should not be over-interpreted.

The selection of any particular strategy or combination of strategies should be determined by a detailed assessment of the students' needs (see Chapter 5). Take as an example a dyslexic child who has demonstrated great difficulty in hearing the component sound units within spoken words. This student, regardless of age, will benefit from activities to enhance phonemic awareness (e.g. identifying sounds, blending sounds, segmenting words into separate phonemes, rhyming and alliteration). Until these skills are established it would be pointless to introduce morphemic or phonic encoding strategies. The phonological skill training must be delivered with a clear focus on the student's particular needs, and must be designed to help bridge the gap between the sound units the student can be taught to identify and the ways in which these sounds may be mapped on to letters. This is of particular importance in the case of young children (Layton *et al.* 1998), but applies also in the case of older students with specific learning difficulties.

Take as another example a child who has reached a temporary plateau at the phonetic stage of development. He or she will be tending to spell many irregular words as if they are phonemically regular, and often will not be aware that the letter sequence written down does not 'look right'. For such a student the strategies listed as Visual Imagery Training, Repeated Writing, and Simultaneous Oral Spelling (SOS) in Figure 2 will all be helpful in establishing an awareness of the visual appearance of a particular word. In a more general way, word study activities such as Word Sorts and Directed Spelling Thinking Activities, using developmentally appropriate vocabulary, will also be helping to establish in the child's long-term memory the immediate recognition of commonly occurring letter clusters in irregular or 'tricky' words. All the above strategies help to take the child smoothly into the transitional stage of spelling.

One important point made clear in Figure 2 is that as the speller moves up through the developmental stages towards independence a wider range of teaching interventions become appropriate for use. Most of the strategies are of value in helping the child progress through the transitional stage to independence. The selection of particular strategies should reflect a detailed knowledge of the specific student's needs (Brooks 1995).

Helping students with learning difficulties: what has research shown?

Can poor spellers become better spellers? This is an important question. Moats (1995) has reached the conclusion that:

> Spelling improvement can be brought about in poor spellers if proper instruction is carried out systematically over a long period of time, and the spelling instruction is tailored to match the developmental level of the student's word knowledge. (p. 89)

Almost 40 studies relating to the teaching of spelling have been carried out over the years, many of them with a particular focus on students with learning difficulties. Some of these studies have been reviewed by Gordon, Vaughn and Schumm (1993), McNaughton, Hughes and Clark (1994), Fulk and Stormont-Spurgin (1995) and Moats (1995). Among the most important conclusions emerging from these reviews are the following.

For students with learning difficulties in spelling:

- Limit the study of words in one session; three words a day appears to bring the best rate of learning and retention.

- Early instruction should focus on high-frequency words and 'easy' words children have misspelled in their own writing.

- Use of different and multisensory response modes can be motivating and can aid assimilation (e.g. writing, tracing, copying using pens of different colour, using plastic letters, keyboarding).

- Some children require up to 40 opportunities to write a word correctly before they have stored it in long-term memory.

- For some students, having them name the letters as they write them at the learning stage is helpful.

- Error imitation, modelling of correct response together with discussion of the differences usually results in improvement.

- Use of computer programs can develop positive attitudes toward drill and practice.

- A few students with poor levels of motivation and confidence may require extrinsic reinforcers to be used at first (e.g. stamps, tokens).

- Peer tutoring and paired learning can be beneficial.

- Teaching students strategies for self-monitoring is essential.

- Revision and periodic re-testing are vital.

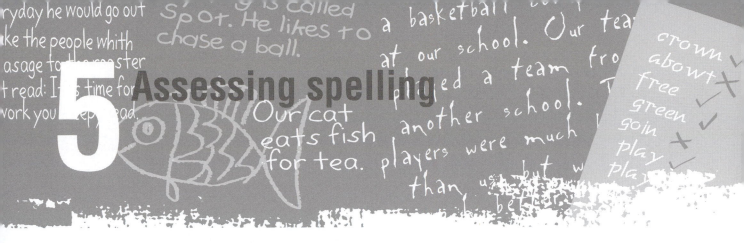

5 Assessing spelling

Assessment in the area of spelling serves the same basic functions as assessment in other areas of the curriculum. These functions include:

- obtaining an indication of the stage of development a particular student has reached;
- identifying any specific weaknesses and special instructional needs the student may have;
- gaining information about what next to teach the student;
- checking on the efficacy of the teaching programme;
- discovering if the student falls into a particular category of special need which entitles him or her to special educational services.

Detailed information concerning a student's spelling skills and strategies is obtained from the following assessment procedures:

- observation of the student while writing;
- analysis of samples of written work;
- reference to benchmark documents and profile guides;
- testing;
- discussions with the student.

Almost all the information teachers need to obtain concerning a student's existing knowledge, skills and strategies in spelling can be obtained by watching the student in action while writing, analysing work samples and talking with the student about his or her insights into the processes of spelling. However, there are occasions when more formal testing of students can provide some additional data to assist programming and reporting.

Observation

Teachers should use observation in a systematic way. Some children will need more frequent attention from the teacher than others, but over a period of weeks the writing and spelling of all children should have been observed (Department for Education and Children's Services (SA) 1997). The observations need to be recorded by the teacher, and, where appropriate, translated into teaching objectives for individual students.

> Direct observation of students as they perform handwriting and spelling activities in their daily assignments provides invaluable diagnostic data. (Miller, Rakes & Choate 1997, p. 215)

Teachers can observe how the students approach the spelling task. For example:

- Are they confident or hesitant?
- Are they willing to take risks and attempt difficult words?
- Do they check and monitor their own spelling?
- Do they self-correct?
- Can they swiftly and easily spell the most commonly needed words?
- Do they help one another with spelling and proofreading?

Information gleaned from observation of children at work needs to be supplemented with information from other sources such as work samples and test results.

Work samples

There is general agreement among experts and practitioners that the most valuable source of information concerning students' spelling ability can be obtained from samples of their unaided writing. By considering the errors a student has made, it is possible to gain some insights into the overall stage of development the student has reached, the knowledge he or she is relying on most when spelling difficult words, and the strategies he or she is using to check and self-correct. It is also possible to observe if any high frequency words are still being misspelt.

Redfern (1993) suggests that the following aspects of spelling should be observed in students' work:

- the relative number of correct spellings;
- the repertoire of common words correctly spelt;
- the visual patterns already known;
- evidence of self-correction;
- any significant error patterns.

Several writers have devised quite complex systems for analysing children's spelling errors (eg. Peters 1975; Howell, Fox & Morehead 1993; Miller, Rakes & Choate 1997). The categories typically include:

- letters omitted (e.g. *rember* for *remember*);
- letters added (e.g. *lotes* for *lots*);
- phonic (including homophones) (e.g. *sed* for *said*; *hear* for *here*);
- phonic but not conforming to rule (e.g. *cyid* for *side*)
- transposition of letters (e.g. *aminal* for animal)
- substitution of a consonant (e.g. *glass* for *class*; *trive* for *drive*);

- substitution of vowel (e.g. *waet* for *wait*)
- double/single letter errors (e.g. *litle* for *little*; *swiming* for *swimming*));
- unclassifiable errors.

Three points concerning error analysis need to be noted here:

- The careful analysis of spelling errors is only worth the time and effort if it leads to some specific form of teaching intervention based on the student's results. It is certainly not a procedure that needs to be applied to any but the most chronic cases of spelling disability.

- In practice it is very difficult to categorise some spelling errors. A single error may appear to fall into several different categories, and an element of subjectivity enters the whole process, thus throwing the final conclusions into question. Inter-scorer agreement is not always high with spelling analyses.

- If only a small sample of errors is available for analysis the reliability of any conclusions reached is suspect. Howell, Fox and Morehead (1993) suggest that at least seventy-five errors are needed to give a reasonably clear picture of a student's existing knowledge and skills.

A highly detailed analysis of spelling errors is usually only required in situations where a student has a specific learning disability, and where individualised tutorial intervention is going to be provided. For general purposes, a less detailed study of work samples will be adequate to allow the teacher to judge the approximate stage of development reached by a student. Analysis of work samples will also allow specific gaps or weaknesses to be identified (for example, too little use made of visual checking strategies; certain high frequency words incorrect; a tendency to add the letter 'e' to the end of words where it is not required). Howell, Fox and Morehead (1993) suggest that when assessing work samples teachers should be on the look out for spelling errors that may actually reflect incorrect, careless or regional speech patterns (for example, word-endings sometimes omitted). They recommend checking the student's ability to say a misspelled word correctly. Gentry (1997) suggests noting whether misspelled words in the child's writing match the difficulty level of the words being studied that week. If the words misspelled in the writing are much more basic than the words in the weekly list, the content of the list may have to be adjusted to a simpler level.

The use of 'portfolios' as a means of collecting and storing students' work samples has become very popular in recent years (Bean 1998; Fiderer 1998). The samples collected should not always be a student's 'best' work as such samples have frequently undergone editing with corrective feedback from the teacher or peers. Some samples should reflect the written work the student can produce unaided. Portfolios might also include a student's test sheets.

Portfolios provide a useful focus for discussions between teachers and students. They can clearly illustrate the student's progress over time, and can highlight aspects of written work still needing attention. Fiderer (1998) suggests that students themselves should also be encouraged to choose work samples to go into their own portfolios and be able to explain why they wish to include those samples. This process helps the students to begin to carry out self-assessment.

Teachers' assessment of work samples is increasingly being related to 'benchmarks' and to 'outcome statements and performance indicators' in such documents as *English: A Curriculum Profile for Australian Schools* (Curriculum Corporation 1994), *Literacy: Professional Elaboration* (Curriculum Corporation 1998) and the *First Steps Spelling Developmental Continuum* (Education Department of Western Australia 1994). These documents provide reasonably clear descriptions of specific knowledge, skills and strategies a student may demonstrate in his or her writing at different stages of development.

Use of benchmarks and profiles

'Benchmarks' usually indicate, in very general terms, what might be expected of most students at a particular age level. For example, a benchmark statement for spelling in Year 3 might be:

Students spell accurately:

1. frequently used and readily recognised words (e.g. *come, going, like, saw, went* and *but*);

2. other one- and two-syllable words:

   a) most monosyllabic words with common spelling patterns, including those with:

   - consonant/consonant digraphs (e.g. *sharp, thick*)
   - vowel/consonant digraphs (e.g. *star, crown*)
   - vowel/vowel digraphs (e.g. *spoon, free*)
   - two-letter consonant blends (e.g. *green, play*)

   b) some words of two syllables with common spelling patterns (e.g. *sunny, playing*)

While students are expected to spell accurately the words described above, they also attempt to spell a wider range of words. Errors made with these words should be phonetically and/or visually plausible approximations to correct spelling (e.g. *gess* for *guess, jungil* for *jungle, redy* for *ready*) (adapted from Curriculum Corporation 1998).

At Year 5 the spelling benchmark might be:

Students spell accurately:

1. most one- and two-syllable words with common spelling patterns, including:
   - all digraphs (e.g. *gr/owing, fou/nd*)
   - some trigraphs (e.g. *might*)
   - two-letter and three-letter consonant blends (e.g. *smooth, scratch*)
   - long vowel sounds (e.g. *date, time*)

2. most of the frequently used and readily recognised words which have less common spelling patterns (e.g. *there, because, who, friends, again*)

3. some other words of more than one syllable (e.g. *yesterday, afternoon, morning, money*).

While students are expected to spell accurately the words described above, they also attempt to spell a wider range of words. Errors made with these words should show students' awareness of phonetic, visual and phonemic patterns (e.g. *accross* for *across*, *comming* for *coming*) and all sounds will be represented (e.g. *finaly* for *finally*) (Curriculum Corporation 1998).

Outcome statements and performance indicators in the English Profiles are different from benchmarks in two respects:

- They are not related to age levels, but refer to the specific types of performance a student of any age might display when he or she has reached, or is reaching, a particular level of development.

- The indicators for any specific learning outcome are usually more detailed than benchmark statements, and can therefore be of more practical value to the teacher when observing students engaged in writing or when assessing work samples.

An example of a typical outcome statement from the English Profiles is:

3.12b (The student) consistently makes informed attempts at spelling. The indicators listed for this outcome are:

- uses new words in writing though unsure of exact spelling;

- uses visual strategies, such as knowledge of letter patterns and critical features of words, to attempt to spell words;

- draws on some spelling generalisations to spell unknown words (use some double letters correctly);

- recognises most misspelt words in own writing and uses variety of resources for correction;

- discusses strategies for spelling difficult words (try a number of ways of spelling a word before deciding which version looks or sounds correct).

The *First Steps Spelling Developmental Continuum* (Education Department of Western Australia 1994) provides some very useful checklists reflecting each of the stages from beginner to independence.

Indicators for spelling outcomes

Towards Level 1

This set of indicators (adapted from Curriculum Corporation 1994) was designed mainly to meet the needs of very young children or those with intellectual and developmental disabilities. This latter group of students are of school age, but not yet able to display skills and strategies within Level 1.

- can grasp writing instrument (or can hit key on keyboard; or point to picture on communication board);
- can make marks on paper (or computer screen);
- can rote copy letters or numerals;
- can identify some common signs in the environment;
- can write first letter of own name;
- can write some letters in own first name;
- can imitate pretend writing when they see others writing;
- shows left to right direction when writing or copying;
- can identify some rhyming words when spoken.

Level 1

At this level the student demonstrates emerging awareness of how to use conventional written symbols for expressing ideas and information.

- can write own first name correctly;
- can sometimes use known or copied words in pretend writing;
- uses letter names and sounds to invent simple spellings;
- can copy letters and words from charts to aid writing;
- can break spoken words down into syllables or onset-rime units;
- can blend sounds aloud to form words;
- can write correctly a small but growing bank of sight words;
- consistently writes from left to right and top to bottom of page.

Level 2

At this level the student uses some basic linguistic structures and features of written language so that writing can be interpreted by others. The student attempts to spell words by drawing mainly on knowledge of sound-symbol relationships and of common letter patterns.

- spells simple high frequency words correctly in own writing;
- spells mainly by matching sounds to known letters/letter clusters;
- shows increasing awareness of syllables in polysyllabic words;
- spells by analogy some simple consonant-vowel-consonant words;
- applies familiar letter pattern to unknown word (e.g. *un-*, *-ed*, *-ing*);

- begins to self-correct own errors in common words;
- knows where and how to obtain help with specific words.

Level 3

At this level the student controls most basic features of written language and consistently makes informed attempts at spelling.

- spells many common words correctly in own writing;
- uses unfamiliar words even though unsure of exact spelling;
- begins to use visual strategies along with phonic strategies;
- recognises most misspelt words in own writing;
- can discuss strategies used for spelling and checking words.

Level 4

At this level the student uses writing as a medium to develop ideas, depict events and record information. The student adjusts writing to take account of aspects of context, purpose and audience, by controlling the linguistic structures and features typical of different genres. The student can also use a range of strategies for planning, writing and editing. In the domain of spelling the student uses a multi-strategy approach.

- displays increasingly efficient proofreading skills;
- recognises and self-corrects most spelling errors by using knowledge of visual features of words, and phonetic and morphemic principles.

Levels 5, 6 and 7

At these more advanced levels of development the student's writing skills for different purposes and for different audiences are well developed. While writing, the spelling of most words is achieved with a high degree of automaticity, although careless errors may still occur. The student has stored a rich supply of word images and letter-strings that can be used smoothly and easily when writing, allowing most cognitive effort to be directed to style and content. This word bank continues to grow as the student engages in more and more reading and writing activities.

In terms of spelling the student:

- proofreads efficiently with aids such as vocabulary lists, dictionary, spell-checker;
- ensures that spelling conforms to standard English;
- displays an increasingly rich vocabulary;
- can describe and demonstrate a variety of strategies for learning and checking the spelling of words.

Testing

It must always be remembered that testing is not teaching. It is only worth using any of the forms of testing referred to below if doing so will yield information that can be applied to the improvement of the teaching programme for individual students. Testing for its own sake is a pointless activity. Used alone, formal and informal testing will never provide a fully comprehensive picture of each student's existing knowledge, skills and strategies. If used appropriately, however, spelling tests can add significantly to the information collected from other sources.

It is sometimes argued that children's spelling achievement in test situations is different from the ability they show when engaged in free writing (Clarke-Klein 1994). Miller, Rakes and Choate (1997) suggest that spelling words correctly on spelling tests is often easier than spelling words correctly in daily written work. Under structured test conditions some students may concentrate on the task and apply spelling knowledge that they don't necessarily use in their free writing. For this reason, appraisal of a child's spelling skills should involve a combination of dictated tests, proofreading tests, and analysis of spelling in spontaneous writing. This point will be discussed more fully in a moment.

Three main types of formal test can be of some value in adding information to that obtained from direct observation and work sample analysis. These forms of test are:

- curriculum-based tests;
- diagnostic tests;
- standardised, norm referenced tests.

Curriculum-based tests

These tests are devised by the teacher and usually contain words that have been the focus of study during the preceding week. They might be thematic words related to some general classroom topic, or they might be a group of words studied to establish understanding of certain phonic units or letter-strings. The purpose of the testing is to determine whether the students have retained the knowledge, or whether revision and re-teaching are necessary. These teacher-made tests can be regarded as 'check-ups', and they form one important part of the formative (on-going) assessment of children's learning.

Diagnostic tests

Diagnostic tests are of particular value when attempting to identify the specific needs of students with learning difficulties. Some diagnostic information can be obtained from curriculum-based tests, from norm referenced tests and from the students' own written work. However, it is often helpful to have available lists of words that allow the teacher to assess in more detail a child's grasp of particular spelling patterns, rules and conventions (see Appendix 4). These diagnostic tools may be teacher-made or may be published test materials. Examples of published diagnostic tests are Croft, Gilmore, Reid & Jackson (1981); Greenbaum (1987); Peters & Smith (1993); Vincent & Claydon (1982); and Vincent & Crumpler (1997) (see Chapter 6).

Teachers would need to examine these diagnostic tests before deciding whether or not information obtained from them could contribute usefully to their own spelling programme. When applying them the teacher is trying to obtain answers to the following three questions:

- What knowledge, skills and strategies does the student already apply when spelling?

- Do any gaps, weaknesses or misunderstandings exist in the student's current repertoire of skills and strategies?

- What does this student, at this developmental level, need to be taught next in order to facilitate further progress?

Examples of informal diagnostic tests are provided in Appendix 4; but as with curriculum-based tests, teachers are able to devise their own tests along similar lines.

Standardised, norm referenced tests

Standardised spelling tests are those tests that have been applied in a standard way to a large representative sample of students in order to determine the average or typical performance of different age groups. This average performance is usually referred to as a 'norm'. Most standardised tests provide tables of norms to permit the comparison of any individual student's performance with that of average students of the same age. The students' performance is usually expressed as a 'spelling age'. For example, a student aged 12 years with difficulties in spelling might be performing at the level of a typical 7-year-old child, so his or her spelling age is given as approximately 7 years.

Standardised tests can be used to screen groups of students to obtain an immediate picture of the spread of ability in a particular class. The results can also be used to identify any students who are having specific difficulties and obviously require additional support.

Some teachers use standardised tests at the beginning and end of each school year as one of their general and quantitative measures of progress made by students. Standardised spelling tests are often used by educational psychologists as part of their psycho-educational assessment of students with learning difficulties.

A limitation of almost all standardised tests of spelling is that they cannot adequately sample the full range of a student's knowledge of word forms, rules and exceptions to rules (Moats 1995). At best, they provide a very rough indication of the level a student has reached. Most spelling tests do allow for an impressionistic judgement to be made as to whether the student is using predominantly a phonetic approach, and how well he or she deals with irregular words

(Moseley 1997). An example of a standardised, norm referenced spelling test, *The South Australian Spelling Test* (1993), is presented in Appendix 3.

The common test formats used for standardised assessment of spelling include:

- dictated spelling lists;
- dictated passages of text;
- proofreading tests (in which the student must identify spelling errors);
- proofreading and correction tests (in which the student must not only identify the errors but must also provide the correct spelling of the words);
- multiple-choice tests (in which the student must select the correct spelling pattern from five or six alternative spellings).

Studies have shown that students' performances across all of these various test formats are highly correlated (Moseley 1997; Westwood 1999). Performance on these tests also tends to be highly correlated with the children's spelling accuracy when writing a story (Westwood 1999). A student's performance in all of the tasks appears to depend upon the same underlying 'general spelling ability' factor identified many years ago by Thurstone (1948).

If the purpose of the standardised testing is to *screen* the overall spelling achievement levels within a class, then any one (or any combination of) the testing formats listed above will tend to rank the children in much the same way. If, however, the purpose of the testing is to obtain a detailed picture of an individual student's existing spelling knowledge and strategies, information from a combination of proofreading, correcting, multiple-choice selecting, and free writing tasks will be required.

Discussion with the student

Some teachers refer to this procedure as 'conferencing'. Time is set aside to allow the teacher to sit with each student to discuss his or her written work. Much of the discussion may focus on the content and style of the writing, but the opportunity to explore the student's spelling and self-correction strategies can also be explored. Some students will require more attention than others in this area.

The teacher and student together can proofread some written work and the teacher can observe the student's skills. The student can be asked such questions as:

- What do you do if you are not quite sure how to spell a word?
- What else could you do?
- How would you sound out this word?

- What do you do if you write a word and it doesn't look right?
- Show me how you might check this word in the dictionary
- Who do you think is a very good speller in this class?
- What do you think helps them to be a good speller?

Sometimes discussions with students can be based on the contents of their writing portfolios. The students can be encouraged to assess their own progress and to identify specific needs for instruction by reference to written work completed at different times and for different purposes. They may, for example, identify particular words which always seem to be giving them problems. These words can be transferred to a personal list of 'spelling demons' to be studied until thoroughly known.

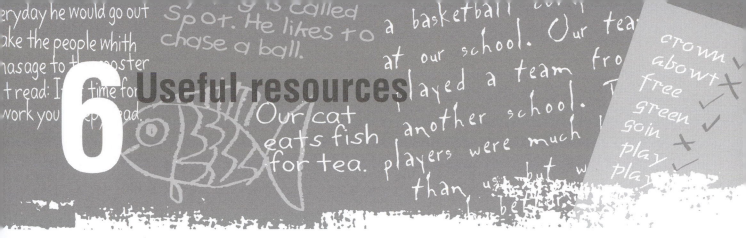

6 Useful resources

Texts

Cheetham, J.S. (1990) *Teach your Child to Spell*. Melbourne: Hyland House. This book describes a step-by-step teaching technique for improving the spelling of any student. The practical suggestions are very helpful for both teachers in schools and to parents at home.

Clutterbuck, P.M. (1990) *The Art of Teaching Spelling*. Melbourne: Longman Cheshire. While stressing the need to have real purposes for writing and spelling the author also provides some very practical suggestions for classroom activities to develop word study techniques. The blackline masters provided in Section 5 may be photocopied. They have great value for overcoming the most common spelling 'demons'. Excellent lists of word families are also provided.

Department for Education and Children's Services (South Australia) (1997) *Spelling: From Beginnings to Independence*. Adelaide: Government Printer. A comprehensive and practical guide to spelling acquisition from the primary years through to adolescence. The approach described in this text takes a developmental perspective and shows how spelling instruction can be integrated into students' reading and writing experiences across the curriculum. Issues of programming, recording and reporting are also discussed.

Gentry, J.R. and Gillet, J. (1993) *Teaching Kids to Spell*. Portsmouth: Heinemann. This book presents a very comprehensive overview of the developmental stages of spelling acquisition, and links assessment and teaching strategies to the stage model. A diagnostic test of ten words can be used to obtain an approximate indication of a child's developmental level from the nature of the errors made. This text is highly recommended.

Mather, N. and Roberts, R. (1995) *Informal Assessment and Instruction in Written Language*. New York: Wiley & Sons. A rich source of instructional methods for the development of spelling skills and the remediation of spelling difficulties. Thirty different procedures and activities are described, most with clearly presented step-by-step instructions.

Moats, L.C. (1995) *Spelling: Development, Disability and Instruction*. Baltimore, MD: York Press. This text is highly recommended. It provides detailed information on the mental processes involved in spelling, and on the links between speech and print. Attention is given to the assessment of spelling ability and to the diagnosis of spelling disabilities. Instructional methods are clearly described. Useful word lists are provided in the appendix. A comprehensive list of references is provided.

Reason, R. and Boote, R. (1994) *Helping Children with Reading and Spelling*. London: Routledge. This text provides a great deal of practical advice for the regular class teacher and the support teacher. Excellent coverage of the development of phonic skills and word study techniques as related to both reading and spelling. Handwriting is also covered.

Redfern, A. (1993) *Practical Ways to Teach Spelling*. Reading: University of Reading. This very concise text (24 pages) contains a useful overview of principles involved in learning to spell. Suggested practices for intervention are related to developmental stages in spelling acquisition. Attention is given to the important issue of developing a whole-school policy on spelling instruction. The book provides a good balance between 'whole language' principles and skills-based instruction.

Treiman, R. (1993) *Beginning to Spell: A Study of First-Grade Children*. New York: Oxford University Press. This extremely comprehensive but fairly technical text represents a very valuable resource for the educational researcher, rather than the practising teacher. The writer presents carefully documented information concerning the developmental stages through which young children progress on their journey to spelling proficiency, with particular reference to the phonological strategies they use and their oral language development. One of Treiman's conclusions is that because reading and spelling do not involve precisely the same processes we cannot assume that spelling ability will simply grow out of reading experience.

Teaching and assessment materials

Andrew, M. (1997) *Reading and Spelling Made Simple* (2nd edn). Melbourne: ACER Press & Gamlen Press. This book offers practical advice and ideas to help students of all ages, particularly those with learning difficulties, to understand the patterns of written English.

Davies, A. and Ritchie, D. (1996) *THRASS (Teaching Handwriting, Reading and Spelling Skills)* London: Collins Educational. This programme is designed to ensure that students in the age range 7 to 11 years (and others with spelling and reading difficulties) acquire a thorough mastery of the way in which the 44 speech sounds (phonemes) in the English language are mapped in print by specific letters or letter clusters (graphemes). The students are helped to understand that in some cases the sound can be represented by a single letter, while in other cases it may require two letters (digraph) or three letters (trigraph). In the area of spelling, the programme enables students to learn thoroughly the alternative ways that the same phoneme may be represented in print by different letter clusters.

Education Department of Western Australia (1994) *First Steps: Spelling Developmental Continuum and Spelling: Resource Book*. Melbourne: Longman. The Developmental Continuum book helps to guide a teacher's assessment of the stage of development reached by each child in the class. The actual sequence of acquisition has been divided into five stages. The Resource Book, as its title suggests, provides many and varied examples of ways in which spelling development can be facilitated in a total literacy programme.

New Zealand Council for Educational Research (1998) *Spell-Write: An Aid to Writing, Spelling and Word Study*. Wellington: NZCER. This material is suitable for school years 3 to 7, and for older students with learning problems. The programme contains the most commonly used 3000+ words in children's writing. The Manual provides information on the concept of spelling, classroom programmes, and evaluating progress in spelling.

Peters, M.L. and Smith, B. (1993) *Spelling in Context*. Windsor: NFER-Nelson. This text places importance on spelling within a conference-process approach to writing, rather than as an isolated subject in its own right, hence the 'in context' part of the title. Many samples of students' writing are provided, both to illustrate developmental stages and to reveal specific strategies being used by the writers. The text also indicates how error analysis can be an important diagnostic aid to planning intervention for individuals. The role of handwriting in facilitating spelling acquisition is discussed. The chapter on strategies for spelling intervention and spelling recovery will be of use to all teachers.

Roberts, J. (1998) *Now I Can Spell! (and Read Better Too)*. Lower Templestowe, Victoria: Learning Pathways. An excellent resource for teachers. This spiral-bound book provides practical suggestions for word games and activities, together with a comprehensive bank of words, word families and dictation passages at each of five levels of complexity.

Rowe, G. and Lomas, B. (1996) *Systematic Spelling: A Classroom Action Plan*. Burwood: Dellasta. A developmental perspective on spelling acquisition has been translated very effectively into a programme. At each of three levels of development the teacher is provided with well-illustrated examples of learning experiences designed to foster optimum progress for students. Assessment of progress is made through the use of checklists of competencies at each level. The book also provides excellent word-banks based on visual, phonemic and morphemic principles. The material is particularly 'user friendly'.

Talbot, V. (1997) *Teaching Reading, Writing and Spelling*. Thousand Oaks, California: Corwin Press. This well-sequenced book of 32 chapters provides some excellent advice on the early teaching of literacy skills, including handwriting and spelling. Sample lessons are provided, and the text is well illustrated. The approach to spelling instruction is mainly from a phonemic/phonics perspective. Beginning teachers in particular will welcome the specific detail contained in curriculum content described by the author.

Vincent, D. and Crumpler, M. (1997) *British Spelling Test Series (BSTS)*. Windsor: NFER-Nelson. These tests can be used from age 5 years to adult level. They can be administered to groups of students or to individuals. Five age levels are covered in each of two parallel forms (approximately 5–9 years; 7–12 years; 10–15.5 years; 12.5–17.5 years; 15.5 years–adult). Several spelling test formats are used (e.g. dictated words, gap filling, dictated passages, proofreading, error detection). The tests are norm referenced, and are useful for screening purposes, monitoring progress over time, and assessing individual students. Results are expressed as standardised scores, spelling ages, percentile ranks, and age-ability scores.

Word study programmes

The following programmes do require that the teacher sets aside specific time each day for word study. The materials are not designed to be integrated easily into a whole language approach. Where these programmes are used, it is essential that the teacher makes every effort to help the students to use the knowledge and skills they have acquired in the programmes when writing, editing and proofreading. As indicated earlier in this book, generalisation of knowledge and skills does not always occur automatically and therefore needs to be facilitated.

Callan, D., Dearsley, R., Paterson, A. and Taylor, P. (1983) Quota *Spelling Program*. Milton, Queensland: Jacaranda. This individualised approach to spelling has been designed to cover Years 1 to 6. One of the basic principles behind the scheme is that each student can measure and record his or her own progress each week. Improvement is judged against individual effort, not against the class average. The basis of the programme is that each student is given an appropriate quota of words to learn each week based on results from pre-tests. The programme allows for the improvement of individual quotas by self effort.

Dixon, R. and Engelmann, S. (1990) *Spelling Mastery*. Chicago: Science Research Associates (and Macmillan-McGraw-Hill). This direct instruction and mastery learning programme is divided into six levels. The programme is generally applicable to students in school years 1 to 6, but can be used with older students who are exhibiting problems in spelling. As the lessons require specific teaching time to be set aside each day (15–20 minutes), and as the words do not come directly from the context of the children's reading and writing, some teachers do not feel comfortable with the programme. Against this perspective it must be recognised that *Spelling Mastery* is very effective in teaching basic phonic knowledge and morphographic principles.

Dixon, R. and Engelmann, S. (1996) *Morphographic Spelling*. Sydney: McGraw-Hill. Morphographic spelling, as its title implies, is a structured programme which explicitly teaches the rules and morphographic principles that govern the ways in which words are constructed. In 140 lessons the students learn all the key morphographs and basic rules of the English spelling system, and practise their application to the point of mastery. The programme is applicable to students from Year 4 upwards, and can also be of value in working with adults. For teachers who themselves have not been taught morphological principles Morphographic Spelling is an invaluable resource. The lessons do require specific teaching time to be set aside each day (15–20 minutes) and spelling is taught as a subject in its own right.

Roser, N. (1995) *SRA Spelling*. Columbus: SRA/McGraw-Hill. A word study programme for Grades 1 to 6. The Teacher's Manual presents a scope and sequence chart indicating the spelling principles covered in each of the year levels. Proofreading, dictionary skills, dictation, puzzles and cloze activities are covered, in addition to the usual exercises in word building.

Appendices

Appendix 1 — Glossary

affix
A meaningful part of a word attached to the beginning (prefix) or end (suffix) of a base or root word.

consonant blend
A two- or three-letter cluster in which the separate sounds are still identifiable but that functions as a useful whole unit for word recognition and spelling: e.g. *st*, *br*, *pl*, *str*.

digraph
Two letters occurring together but representing only one phoneme (speech sound): e.g. *sh*, *th*, *ch*, *wh*, *ng*, *ea*.

diphthong
A vowel that has two distinct sounds with a 'slide' or shift in the middle, e.g. *oy* in *boy*.

grapheme
A letter or cluster of letters representing one speech sound.

grapho-phonic
Correspondence between written or printed symbols and the sound units they represent (see also *phonics*).

homonyms
Words with the same spelling pattern but different meaning.

homophones
Words which sound the same but are spelt differently.

morpheme
The smallest unit of meaning in spoken and written language.

morphograph
The written equivalent of a morpheme.

onset
The initial sound in a syllable occurring before the vowel (*p* - *ot*).

orthography
The writing and spelling system. Orthographic knowledge can be regarded as stored information about the regularities and exceptionalities of the spelling system. 'Orthographic processing skill' is the ability to use such information in a range of reading and spelling tasks (Holmes 1996, p.149).

phoneme
A speech sound.

phonemic awareness
The ability to detect differences and similarities among speech sounds, to segment words into separate sound units, and to identify and blend sequences of speech sounds (also *phoneme blending*).

phonics	The system that establishes connection between speech sounds and symbols (also *phonic approach* to reading).
phonogram	A written spelling pattern made up from a particular cluster of letters.
phonology	The body of knowledge dealing with the speech sound components of a language.
rime	The last part of a syllable; the vowel and all the letters that follow it.
trigraph	A unit of three letters representing only one speech sound (e.g. *-igh*, *-eau*).

125 most commonly used words in children's writing

a	come	here	of	them
about	could	him	off	then
after	dad	his	on	there
all	day	home	one	they
am	did	house	only	this
an	do	I	or	time
and	dog	if	our	to
are	doing	in	out	took
as	down	into	outside	two
at	egg	is	over	up
away	first	it	play	very
baby	for	just	played	was
back	friend	like	playing	we
ball	from	liked	put	went
be	get	little	ran	were
because	girl	look	said	what
bed	go	made	saw	when
been	going	make	school	where
big	good	me	see	which
but	got	more	she	who
by	had	mum	so	will
called	has	my	some	with
came	have	no	that	would
can	he	not	the	you
children	her	now	their	your

For a more comprehensive list see Graham, Harris and Loynachan (1994). For a list arranged according to frequency in children's writing see Croft (1998).

Source: adapted from Huxford, McGonagle & Warren 1997; Snowball 1997b)

63

Appendix 3

South Australian Spelling Test (SAST)

The South Australian Spelling Test (SAST) is a standardised test of spelling achievement for students in the age range 6 years to 15 years. SAST is based on a graded word list compiled by Dr Margaret Peters of Cambridge University. The main purpose of the test is to provide a quick screening instrument to enable teachers to determine the spread of spelling ability in their classes and to identify students who require additional help. The test can also be used before and after any specific intervention program designed to improve students' spelling skills. Used in this way the test provides a quantitative measure of the progress made by the students which can accompany the more descriptive or qualitative assessments based on students' written work samples and the English Profiles.

Close inspection of the errors a student makes in the spelling test can also yield some limited diagnostic information. For example, it is possible to note the individual's ability to spell phonetically, to use syllabification, to spell some irregular words, and to produce certain common letter-strings. Used together with other sources of information, performance on the test may help a teacher to determine the developmental stage a child has reached in the acquisition of spelling skills.

The test can be administered orally to an individual student or to a whole class. A written response is required from the student and the results are scored as either correct or incorrect.

A student's raw score (total of items correct) can be evaluated against the range of scores typical for students of that particular age level (see Table1). The raw score can also be converted into an approximate spelling age for that student (see Table 2).

Technical details

The test, originally standardised on children in England, was also normed on large representative samples of South Australian children in 1978 and again in 1993. Table 1 and Table 2 provide norms based on the testing of 10, 613 South Australian children in 1993.

- The test-retest reliability of the South Australian Spelling Test is .96 for students in the primary school age range (Year 3 to Year 7).

- The standard error of measurement is approximately ± 2 marks on raw score.

- The Normal Range of Scores for each age level was based on the spread of scores reflecting the performance of 50% of the age group. This was calculated on ± .68 standard deviation. These scores have been rounded to the nearest whole number in Table 1.

- The Critically Low Score has been calculated on the basis that 10% of the age group would fall 1.29 standard deviations below the mean.

South Australian Spelling Test (SAST)

1.	ON	Please put your shoe ON. Write ON.
2.	HOT	The water in the bath is HOT. Write HOT.
3.	CUP	I drink from a CUP. Write CUP.
4.	VAN	The lady can drive the VAN. Write VAN.
5.	JAM	I like JAM on my bread. Write JAM.
6.	LOST	I LOST my key. Write LOST.
7.	SIT	Please SIT on this chair. Write SIT.
8.	PLAN	I used a PLAN to make this model. Write PLAN.
9.	MUD	I got MUD on my shoes when it rained. Write MUD.
10.	BEG	I taught my dog to BEG for a biscuit. Write BEG.
11.	THE	Is this THE toy you want? Write THE.
12.	GO	I will GO to the shops after school. Write GO.
13.	FOR	Is this letter FOR me? Write FOR.
14.	SO	You did that job SO quickly. Write SO.
15.	ME	This present is not for ME. Write ME.
16.	ARE	Animals ARE in the field. Write ARE.
17.	OF	I am not sure OF your name. Write OF.
18.	DO	What will you DO next? Write DO.
19.	WHO	WHO was that knocking at the door? Write WHO.
20.	HERE	Put the box over HERE. Write HERE.
21.	SHIP	A SHIP is on the sea. Write SHIP.
22.	CHOP	The butcher will CHOP the meat. Write CHOP.
23.	FOOD	We must take FOOD to the picnic. Write FOOD.
24.	FIRE	We need dry sticks to start the FIRE. Write FIRE.
25.	THIN	The THIN cat squeezed under the fence. Write THIN.
26.	DATE	What is the DATE today? Write DATE.
27.	SEEM	The shop did not SEEM to be open. Write SEEM.
28.	DART	I threw a DART at the dartboard. Write DART.
29.	LOUD	Your voice is too LOUD. Write LOUD.
30.	FROM	Our new teacher comes FROM Sydney. Write FROM.
31.	EYE	Please shut one EYE and look at this. Write EYE.
32.	FIGHT	I saw two dogs FIGHT in the park. Write FIGHT.
33.	FRIEND	She is my best FRIEND. Write FRIEND.
34.	DONE	What have you DONE with your book? Write DONE.
35.	ANY	Are there ANY cakes left? Write ANY.

36.	GREAT	I was chased by a GREAT big dog. Write GREAT.
37.	SURE	I am not SURE how to spell this. Write SURE
38.	WOMEN	Two WOMEN went for a swim. Write SWIM.
39.	ANSWER	Please ANSWER my question. Write ANSWER.
40.	BEAUTIFUL	The flowers in the garden look BEAUTIFUL.
41.	ORCHESTRA	I play the piano in the ORCHESTRA.
42.	EQUALLY	They shared the money EQUALLY.
43.	APPRECIATE	Thank you. I APPRECIATE your help.
44.	FAMILIAR	His face seemed FAMILIAR. Had we met before?
45.	ENTHUSIASTIC	The student was an ENTHUSIASTIC player.
46.	SIGNATURE	She wrote her SIGNATURE on the paper.
47.	BREATHE	Fresh air is good to BREATHE.
48.	PERMANENT	Will that sign be taken away or is it PERMANENT?
49.	SUFFICIENT	We have SUFFICIENT food to last for the weekend.
50.	SURPLUS	We will sell the SURPLUS apples. We have too many.
51.	CUSTOMARY	It is CUSTOMARY to shake hands.
52.	ESPECIALLY	This gift is ESPECIALLY for you.
53.	MATERIALLY	This story is not MATERIALLY different from the one in your book.
54.	CEMETERY	The funeral took place at the CEMETERY.
55.	LEISURE	She spent her LEISURE time in the garden.
56.	FRATERNALLY	FRATERNALLY means the same as brotherly.
57.	SUCCESSFUL	The fund-raising was very SUCCESSFUL.
58.	DEFINITE	I agreed on a DEFINITE time to meet her.
59.	EXHIBITION	There is an art EXHIBITION at the gallery.
60.	APPARATUS	We use this APPARATUS in the science lab.
61.	MORTGAGE	I bought the house by taking a MORTGAGE.
62.	EQUIPPED	The campers were EQUIPPED with new tents.
63.	SUBTERRANEAN	SUBTERRANEAN means under the ground.
64.	POLITICIAN	Did you vote for that POLITICIAN?
65.	MISCELLANEOUS	Mixing different items together makes a MISCELLANEOUS set.
66.	EXAGGERATE	The fish wasn't that big! Don't EXAGGERATE.
67.	GUARANTEE	My washing machine has a two-year GUARANTEE.
68.	EMBARRASSING	I find it EMBARRASSING to give a speech.
69.	CONSCIENTIOUS	Students who work hard are said to be CONSCIENTIOUS.
70.	SEISMOGRAPH	A SEISMOGRAPH is an instrument to measure the strength of earthquakes.

Instructions for administration

1. Students should be seated in a position where copying from others is not possible.

2. Each student requires a sheet of paper and pen or pencil.

3. Students should number each item before writing the response.

4. Students should be encouraged to attempt as many items as possible; but with young children, or students with learning difficulties, do not prolong the test unnecessarily.

5. It is usual to stop testing after a student has failed ten *consecutive* items.

6. When marking do not give credit for any words beyond the tenth *consecutive* error.

7. When marking do not penalise for reversals of *b* and *d*.

8. The method of administration is to say the number of the item. Then say the word clearly. Embed the word in a sentence. Then repeat the word, saying for example: 'Number 6: *lost*. I *lost* my key. Write *lost*.'

9. If any of the sentences suggested here appear inappropriate for the age or ability level being tested they can be changed by the tester provided that the sense of the word is retained.

Interpretation of scores

The student's raw score is obtained by counting the number of items correct on his or her test sheet. No credit should be given for correct responses occurring after *a block of ten consecutive errors*.

Table 1 allows the teacher to compare a student's raw score with the average score obtained by other students of the same age. It is also possible to determine whether the student is performing within the 'normal' range of scores for his or her age level, or whether the score is critically low. 'Normal' range indicates the spread of scores within which 50% of the students of that age score. The critically low score represents the score below which only 10% of the age group would be scoring. Students in the critically low group almost certainly need additional support from the teacher in order to develop more effective spelling strategies.

Examples:
1. A girl aged 10 years 0 months scores 42 on the SAST. This places her just within the upper range of 'normal' performance for students of that age. Her score is slightly above average.

2. Her friend, also age 10 years 0 months, scores only 26. This places her in the bottom 10% of students of that age. It would be important to analyse the errors this student makes in order to determine where special assistance can best be directed.

Referring to Table 2 below, the *spelling age* for each of the two students just described is approximately 11.2 years and 7.6 years respectively.

When using Table 2 it is important to apply the known Standard Error of Measurement of the SAST (±2 points). It would be more accurate to describe the spelling ages of the two students referred to above as follows:
(Girl 1) 42 - 2 = 40 and 42 + 2 = 44.
Spelling ages for scores of 40 and 44 are 10.7 years to 11.7 years.
The spelling age for Girl 1 is within the range 10. 7 to 11.7 years.

(Girl 2) 26 - 2 = 24 and 26 + 2 = 28. Reading from Table 2, the spelling age for Girl 2 is between 7.3 years and 8.0 years.

Table 1: Ages, average scores, normal ranges and critically low scores

Students' Age (yrs/mths)	Average Score	Normal Range	Critically Low Score	Students' Age (yrs/mths)	Average Score	Normal Range	Critically Low Score	Students' Age (yrs/mths)	Average Score	Normal Range	Critically Low Score
6.0	14	8 – 20	4	9.3	34	28 – 40	24	12.6	47	40 – 54	37
6.1	15	9 – 21	5	9.4	35	29 – 41	25	12.7	47	40 – 54	37
6.2	15	9 – 21	5	9.5	35	29 – 41	25	12.8	48	41 – 55	38
6.3	16	10 – 22	6	9.6	35	29 – 41	25	12.9	48	41 – 55	38
6.4	16	10 – 22	6	9.7	36	30 – 42	26	12.10	48	41 – 55	38
6.5	17	11 – 23	7	9.8	36	30 – 42	26	12.11	48	41 – 55	38
6.6	18	12 – 24	8	9.9	36	30 – 42	26	13.0	48	41 – 55	38
6.7	18	12 – 24	8	9.10	37	31 – 43	27	13.1	48	41 – 55	38
6.8	19	13 – 25	9	9.11	37	31 – 43	27	13.2	48	41 – 55	38
6.9	19	13 – 25	9	10.0	37	31 – 43	27	13.3	48	41 – 55	38
6.10	20	14 – 26	10	10.1	37	31 – 43	27	13.4	48	41 – 55	38
6.11	21	15 – 27	11	10.2	38	32 – 44	28	13.5	48	41 – 55	38
7.0	22	16 – 28	12	10.3	38	32 – 44	28	13.6	48	41 – 55	38
7.1	22	16 – 28	12	10.4	38	32 – 44	28	13.7	49	42 – 56	39
7.2	23	17 – 29	13	10.5	39	33 – 44	29	13.8	49	42 – 56	39
7.3	23	17 – 29	13	10.6	39	34 – 44	29	13.9	49	42 – 56	39
7.4	24	18 – 30	14	10.7	40	35 – 45	30	13.10	49	42 – 56	39
7.5	24	18 – 30	14	10.8	40	35 – 45	30	13.11	50	43 – 57	40
7.6	25	19 – 31	15	10.9	40	35 – 45	30	14.0	50	43 – 57	40
7.7	25	19 – 31	15	10.10	41	35 – 47	31	14.1	50	43 – 57	40
7.8	26	20 – 32	16	10.11	41	35 – 47	31	14.2	50	43 – 57	40
7.9	27	21 – 33	17	11.0	41	35 – 47	31	14.3	50	43 – 57	40
7.10	27	21 – 33	17	11.1	42	36 – 48	32	14.4	51	45 – 57	41
7.11	28	22 – 34	18	11.2	42	36 – 48	32	14.5	51	45 – 57	41
8.0	28	22 – 34	18	11.3	42	36 – 48	32	14.6	51	45 – 57	41
8.1	29	23 – 35	19	11.4	43	39 – 49	33	14.7	51	45 – 57	41
8.2	29	23 – 35	19	11.5	43	39 – 49	33	14.8	51	45 – 57	41
8.3	30	24 – 36	20	11.6	44	38 – 50	34	14.9	51	45 – 57	41
8.4	30	24 – 36	20	11.7	44	38 – 50	34	14.10	52	46 – 58	42
8.5	31	25 – 37	21	11.8	44	38 – 50	34	14.11	52	46 – 58	42
8.6	31	25 – 37	21	11.9	44	38 – 50	34	15.0	52	46 – 58	42
8.7	31	26 – 36	21	11.10	45	39 – 51	35	15.1	52	46 – 58	42
8.8	32	26 – 37	22	11.11	45	39 – 51	35	15.2	52	46 – 58	42
8.9	32	26 – 38	22	12.0	45	39 – 51	35	15.3	52	46 – 58	42
8.10	32	26 – 38	22	12.1	46	40 – 52	36	15.4	52	46 – 58	42
8.11	33	27 – 39	23	12.2	46	40 – 52	36	15.5	52	46 – 58	42
9.0	33	27 – 39	23	12.3	46	40 – 52	36	15.6	52	46 – 58	42
9.1	33	27 – 39	23	12.4	47	40 – 54	37				
9.2	34	28 – 40	24	12.5	47	40 – 54	37				

Source: South Australian Spelling Test, norms, 1993

Table 2: Approximate spelling ages

Raw Score	Approx. Spelling Age	Raw Score	Approx. Spelling Age
12	below 6.0 yrs	33	9.0 yrs
13	6.0 yrs	34	9.2 yrs
14	6.0 yrs	35	9.5 yrs
15	6.1 yrs	36	9.7 yrs
16	6.3 yrs	37	10.0 yrs
17	6.4 yrs	38	10.2 yrs
18	6.5 yrs	39	10.5 yrs
19	6.7 yrs	40	10.7 yrs
20	6.8 yrs	41	10.9 yrs
21	6.9 yrs	42	11.2 yrs
22	7.1 yrs	43	11.4 yrs
23	7.2 yrs	44	11.7 yrs
24	7.3 yrs	45	12.0 yrs
25	7.5 yrs	46	12.2 yrs
26	7.6 yrs	47	12.4 yrs
27	7.8 yrs	48	13.0 yrs
28	8.0 yrs	49	13.8 yrs
29	8.2 yrs	50	14.2 yrs
30	8.4 yrs	51	14.5 yrs
31	8.6 yrs	52	15.5 yrs
32	8.9 yrs	53	above 15.5 yrs

Source: South Australian Spelling Test, 1993

Notes:

1. Note that spelling ages are in years and tenths of a year (not months).
2. Apply Standard Error of Measurement + 2 and - 2 points on raw score.

   Example: Child scores 26 marks.
   - Subtract 2 from 26 = 24.
   - Add 2 to 26 = 28.
   - Enter table at raw score 24 and at 28.

   Thus the child's spelling age is between 7.3 years and 8.0 years.

Diagnostic tests

Diagnostic test A: Some predictable spelling patterns

The words in the list below may be used as a quick assessment of a student's ability to spell dictated words that are reasonably regular in terms of letter (or letter cluster) to sound correspondences. The test also provides an opportunity to examine the student's grasp of a selection of consonant blends and digraphs used in the initial and final position. Any student who performs poorly on the first thirty words should be checked for basic phonological awareness and phonic knowledge (see Diagnostic Test D).

The final two words in each column require knowledge of syllable units.

at	if	on	up	wet
bag	rod	fin	bus	men
chop	plot	ship	trap	step
flag	swim	glad	drop	slug
must	risk	silk	send	lamp
fact	help	sift	luck	song
scrap	string	split	think	shack
winter	person	driving	action	beside
freedom	latest	project	chapter	remember

Diagnostic test B: Some less predictable words

With this test it is important to observe how the student goes about the task of attempting to spell these words. Are the errors mainly phonetic?

the	ask	are	any	does
said	sure	was	they	come
tough	work	master	half	lawn
laugh	wander	glove	women	where

Diagnostic test C: Core list of hard-to-spell words

These words (or some of them) can be given as a test. Students who cannot spell any of these words should write the correct spelling on a personal reference card, and use this card when proofreading.

an	of	all	it's	off
saw	too	two	was	came
come	hour	into	kept	knew
know	said	then	they	want
went	were	when	again	could
heard	might	right	still	that's
their	there	tried	until	where
always	bought	caught	friend	houses
inside	myself	opened	people	played
police	school	turned	another	decided
outside	running	started	stopped	thought
through	because	suddenly	sometimes	

Source: Moseley 1997. Reproduced with the author's permission

Diagnostic test D: Test of basic phonic knowledge

In the case of very young children, or older students with learning problems, it is often useful to check that they know the most common letter-to-sound correspondences. Any gaps detected in their basic phonic knowledge can then be identified easily and remedied.

Present each of the following letters (capital and lower case) on separate cards and ask the child to say the letter name and letter sound. The activity can be played as a game.

B	H	F	K	P	W	A	O	J	U	C	Y	M
Q	Z	L	N	S	T	R	I	G	E	V	D	X
f	k	w	p	z	a	g	h	b	j	u	c	y
q	l	i	m	d	n	s	t	r	v	e	o	x

If students know the most common sounds associated with single letters as above, card material or a checklist can be used to determine their ability to recognise and blend two sounds and to recognise common digraphs, trigraphs, and consonant blends.

ab	ad	ag	am	an	ap	at	ed	eg
en	et	ib	id	ig	in	ip	it	ob
od	og	op	ot	ub	ug	um	un	up
ut	ch	sh	th	ph	wh	ck	wr	bl
br	cl	cr	dr	fl	gl	gr	st	sp
sw	pl	pr	tr	sm	sl	fr	sn	sk
sc	tw	str	scr	spr	thr	spl	shr	squ

If a student has clearly developed beyond the basic phonic stages represented above, he or she can be checked for recognition of common letter strings such as those listed below. As well as being able to say the sound unit represented by the letter group, the student can be asked to think of some words containing that unit and to write the words.

amp	ump	and	end	ast	est	ist
ust	ank	ink	all	ill	ull	ang
ant	ent	int	unt	old	alk	ilk
elt	ilt	atch	itch	unch	uch	act
ift	ong	orm	orn	ulk	umb	oss
ar	ay	ea	ey	ure	er	ow
dge	tch	eer	igh			

References

Adams, M.J. (1990) *Beginning to Read: Thinking and Learning About Print*. Cambridge, MA: MIT Press.

Andrews, S. and Scarratt, D. (1996) What comes after phonological awareness? Using lexical experts to investigate orthographic processes in reading. *Australian Journal of Psychology, 48, 3*, 141-148.

Arvidson, G.L. (1969) *Learning to Spell*. Wellington: New Zealand Council for Educational Research.

Ball, E.W. and Blachman, B.A. (1991) Does phonemic awareness training in kindergarten make a difference in early word recognition and developmental spelling? *Reading Research Quarterly, 27*, 49-66.

Barone, D. (1992) Whatever happened to spelling? The role of spelling instruction in process-centered classrooms. *Reading Psychology, 13, 1*, 1-17.

Bartch, J. (1992) An alternative to spelling: an integrated approach. *Language Arts, 69*, 404-408.

Bean, W. (1998) Spelling across the grades. In J. Coombs (ed.) *Getting Started: Ideas for the Literacy Teacher*. Newton, NSW: Primary English Teaching Association.

Bell, N. (1991) *Visualizing and Verbalizing*. Paso Robles, CA: Academy of Reading Publications.

Berninger, V.W., Abbott, R.D., Whitaker, D., Sylvester, L. and Nolen, S.B. (1995) Integrating low and high-level skills in instructional protocols for writing disabilities. *Learning Disabilities Quarterly, 18, 4*, 293-309.

Bissex, G. (1980) *Gnys at Wrk*. Cambridge, MA: Harvard University Press.

Bouffler, C. (1997) They don't teach spelling any more—or do they? *Australian Journal of Language and Literacy, 20, 2*, 140-147.

Bradley, L. (1983) The organisation of visual, phonological, and motor strategies in learning to read and spell. In U. Kirk (ed.) *Neuropsychology of Language, Reading and Spelling*. New York: Academic Press.

Bradley, L. (1990) Rhyming connections in learning to read and spell. In P.D. Pumfrey and C.D. Elliott (eds) *Children's Difficulties in Reading, Spelling and Writing*. London: Falmer.

Brann, B. (1997) Analysis of spelling attempts: the Brann Analysis Grid for Spelling. In D. Greaves and P. Jeffery (eds) *Learning Difficulties, Disabilities and Resource Teaching*. Melbourne: The Australian Resource Educators' Association.

Brooks, P. (1995) The effectiveness of various teaching strategies in the teaching of spelling to a student with severe specific difficulties. *Educational and Child Psychology, 12, 1*, 8-88.

Bryant, P. and Bradley, L. (1980) Why children sometimes write words which they do not read. In U. Frith (ed.) *Cognitive Processes in Spelling*. New York: Academic Press.

Bryant, P. and Bradley, L. (1985) *Children's Reading Problems*. Oxford: Blackwell.

Butyniec-Thomas, J. and Woloshyn, V.E. (1997) The effects of explicit strategy and whole-language instruction on students' spelling ability. *Journal of Experimental Education*, *65, 4,* 293-302.

Cambourne, B. (1988) *The Whole Story: Natural Learning and Literacy Acquisition.* Auckland: Ashton Scholastic.

Candlin, C.N. (1997) Preface. In D. Butt, R. Fahey, S. Spinks and C. Yallop (eds) *Using Functional Grammar: An Explorer's Guide.* Sydney: Macquarie University.

Cataldo, S. and Ellis, N. (1990) Learning to spell, learning to read. In P.D. Pumfrey and C.D. Elliott (eds) *Children's Difficulties in Reading, Spelling and Writing.* London: Falmer.

Clark, D.B. and Uhry, J.K. (1995) *Dyslexia: Theory and Practice of Remedial Instruction.* Baltimore: York Press.

Clark, J.M. and Paivio, A. (1991) Dual coding theory and education. *Educational Psychology Review*, *3, 3,* 149-210.

Clarke-Klein, S.M. (1994) Expressive phonological deficiencies: impact on spelling development. *Topics in Language Disorders*, *14, 2,* 40-55.

Coltheart, V. and Leahy, J. (1996) Procedures used by beginning and skilled readers to read unfamiliar letter strings. *Australian Journal of Psychology*, *48, 3,* 124-129.

Cripps, C. (1990) Teaching joined writing to children on school entry as an agent for catching spelling. *Australian Journal of Remedial Education*, *22, 3,* 13-15.

Croft, C. (1998) *Spell-Write: An Aid to Writing, Spelling and Word Study.* Wellington: New Zealand Council for Educational Research.

Cunningham, P.M. (1998) The multisyllabic word dilemma: helping students build meaning, spell and read 'big' words. *Reading and Writing Quarterly*, *14, 2,* 189-218.

Curriculum Corporation (1994) *English: A Curriculum Profile for Australian Schools.* Melbourne: Curriculum Corporation.

Curriculum Corporation (1998) *Literacy: Professional Elaboration.* Melbourne: Curriculum Corporation.

Dale, E., O'Rourke, J. and Barbe, W. (1986) *Vocabulary Building: A Process Approach.* Columbus: Zaner-Bloser.

Davies, A. and Ritchie, D. (1996) *Teaching Handwriting, Reading and Spelling Skills (THRASS).* London: HarperCollins.

Department for Education and Children's Services (South Australia) (1997) *Spelling: From Beginnings to Independence.* Adelaide: Government Printer.

Dixon, R.C. (1991) The application of sameness analysis to spelling. *Journal of Learning Disabilities*, *24, 5,* 285-291.

Dixon, R. and Engelmann, S. (1976) *Morphographic Spelling.* Sydney: SRA/McGraw-Hill.

Dixon, R. and Engelmann, S. (1990) *Spelling Mastery.* Sydney: SRA/McGraw-Hill.

Dougherty, S. and Clayton, M. (1998) The effect on spelling ability of exposure to the printed word. *Research in Education*, *59,* 80-94.

Education Department of Western Australia (1994) *First Steps: Spelling Developmental Continuum.* Melbourne: Longman Cheshire.

Ehri, L. (1989) Development of spelling knowledge and its role in reading acquisition and reading disabilities. *Journal of Learning Disabilities*, *22*, 356-370.

Elbro, C. and Arnbak, E. (1996) The role of morpheme recognition and morphological awareness in dyslexia. *Annals of Dyslexia*, *46*, 209-240.

Ellis. A.W. (1984) *Reading, Writing and Dyslexia: A Cognitive Analysis*. London: Erlbaum.

Fiderer, A. (1998) Assessing literacy levels in your classroom. *Classroom*, *98*, *2*, 18-19.

Fox, M. (1997) Towards a personal theory of whole language: a teacher-researcher-writer reflects. *Australian Journal of Language and Literacy*, *20*, *2*, 122-130.

Fulk, B.M. (1996) The effects of combined strategy and attribution training on LD adolescents' spelling performance. *Exceptionality*, *6*, *1*, 13-27

Fulk, B.M. (1997) Think while you spell: a cognitive motivational approach to spelling instruction. *Teaching Exceptional Children*, *29*, *4*, 70-71.

Fulk, B.M. and Stormont-Spurgin, M. (1995) Spelling interventions for students with disabilities: a review. *The Journal of Special Education*, *28*, *4*, 488-513.

Gagne, R., Briggs, L. and Wager, W. (1992) *Principles of Instructional Design* (4th edn). Chicago: Holt, Rinehart and Winston.

Gagne, E., Yekovich, C. and Yekovich, F. (1993) *The Cognitive Psychology of School Learning* (2nd edn). New York: HarperCollins.

Gaskins, I., Ehri, L., Cress, C., O'Hara, C. and Donnelly, K. (1997a) Analyzing words and making discoveries about the alphabetic system: activities for beginning readers. *Language Arts*, *74*, *3*, 172-184.

Gaskins, I., Ehri, L., Cress, C., O'Hara, C. and Donnelly, K. (1997b) Procedures for word learning: making discoveries about words. *The Reading Teacher*, *50*, *4*, 312-327.

Gentry, J.R. (1981) Learning to spell developmentally. *The Reading Teacher*, *34*, *4*, 378-381.

Gentry, J.R. (1997) Spelling strategies. *Instructor*, *107*, *4*, 56-57.

Gentry, J.R. and Gillet, J.W. (1993) *Teaching Kids to Spell*. Portsmouth, NH: Heinemann.

Gerber, M.M. (1986) Generalization of spelling strategies by learning disabled students as a result of contingent imitation-modelling and mastery criteria. *Journal of Learning Disabilities*, *19*, 530-537.

Gillingham, A. and Stillman, B. (1960) *Remedial Teaching for Children with Specific Disability in Reading, Spelling and Penmanship*. Cambridge, MA: Educators Publishing Service.

Goodman, K.S. (1986) *What's Whole in Whole Language?* Portsmouth, NJ: Heinemann.

Gordon, J., Vaughn, S. and Schumm, J. (1993) Spelling interventions: a review of literature and implications for instruction for students with learning disabilities. *Learning Disabilities: Research and Practice*, *8*, *3*, 175-181.

Goswami, U. (1992) Annotation: phonological factors in spelling development. *Journal of Child Psychology and Psychiatry*, *33*, *6*, 967-975.

Graham, S. and Freeman, S. (1985) Strategy training and teacher vs student-controlled study conditions: effects on LD students spelling performance. *Learning Disability Quarterly*, *8*, 267-274.

Graham, S. and Harris, K.R. (1994) Implications of constructivism for teaching writing to students with special needs. *Journal of Special Education*, *28*, *3*, 275-289.

Graham, S., Harris, K. and Loynachan, C. (1994) The spelling for writing list. *Journal of Learning Disabilities*, *27*, *4*, 210-214.

Graham, S., Harris, K. and Loynachan, C. (1996) The Directed Spelling Thinking Activity: application with high-frequency words. *Learning Disabilities: Research and Practice*, *11*, *1*, 34-40.

Grainger, J. (1997) *Children's Behaviour, Attention and Reading Problems*. Melbourne: ACER Press.

Greenbaum, C.R. (1987) *Spellmaster: An Assessment and Teaching System*. Austin, TX: ProEd.

Gunning, T.G. (1995) Word building: a strategic approach to the teaching of phonics. *The Reading Teacher*, *48*, *6*, 484-488.

Harrison, B., Zollner, J. and Magill, B. (1996) The hole in whole language. *Australian Journal of Remedial Education*, *27*, *5*, 6-18.

Hewson, J. (1990) Paired spelling. *Support for Learning*, *5*, *3*, 136-140.

Hoffman, P.R. (1990) Spelling, phonology, and the speech-language pathologist: a whole language perspective. *Language, Speech and Hearing Services in Schools*, *21*, 238-243.

Holmes, V.M. (1996) Skilled reading and orthographic processing. *Australian Journal of Psychology*, *48*, *3*, 149-154.

Howell, K., Fox, S. and Morehead, M. (1993) *Curriculum-based evaluation* (2nd edn). Pacific Grove: Brooks-Cole.

Hutton, D. and Lescohier, J.A. (1983) Seeing to learn: using mental imagery in the classroom. In M.L. Fleming and D.W. Hutton (eds) *Mental Imagery and Learning*. Englewood Cliffs, NJ: Educational Technology Publications.

Huxford, L., McGonagle, R. and Warren, S. (1997) Which words? Words which 4- to 6-year-old children use in their writing. *Reading*, *31*, *3*, 16-21.

Invernizzi, M., Abouzeid, M. and Gill, J.T. (1994) Using students' invented spellings as a guide for spelling instruction that emphasizes word study. *Elementary School Journal*, *95*, *2*, 155-167.

Jongsma, K.S. (1990) Reading-Spelling links. *The Reading Teacher*, *43*, *8*, 608-609.

Jorm, A. (1983) *The Psychology of Reading and Spelling Disability*. London: Routledge.

Layton, L., Deeny, K., Upton, G. and Tall, G. (1998) A pre-school training programme for children with poor phonological awareness: effects on reading and spelling. *Journal of Research in Reading*, *21*, *1*, 36 – 52.

Leary, G. and Johncock, W. (1995) Using computers in the classroom to develop spelling skills. In R. Oliver and M. Wild (eds) *Learning Without Limits*. Proceedings of the Australian Computers in Education Conference. Claremont, WA: Educational Computing Association.

Lowe, K. and Walters, J. (1991) The unsuccessful reader: negotiating new perceptions. In E. Furniss and P. Green (eds) *The Literacy Agenda: Issues for the Nineties*. Melbourne; Eleanor Curtin Publishing.

Lyndon, H. (1989) I did it my way. An introduction to Old Way-New Way. *Australasian Journal of Special Education*, *13*, 32-37.

MacArthur, C.A., Graham, S., Haynes, J.B. and DeLaPaz, S. (1996) Spelling checkers and students with learning disabilities: performance comparisons and impact on spelling. *Journal of Special Education*, 30, 1, 35-57.

McCoy, K. (1995) *Teaching Special Learners in the General Education Classroom* (2nd edn). Denver: Love.

McLaughlin, T.F. and Skinner, C.H. (1996) Improving academic performance through self-management: cover, copy and compare. *Intervention in School and Clinic*, 32, 2, 113-118.

McNaughton, D., Hughes, C. and Clark, K. (1994) Spelling instruction for students with learning disabilities: implications for research and practice. *Learning Disability Quarterly*, 17, 3, 169-185.

Mather, N. and Roberts, R. (1995) *Informal Assessment and Instruction in Written Language*. New York: Wiley.

Miller, L.J., Rakes, T.A. and Choate, J.S. (1997) Handwriting and spelling: tools for communication. In J.S. Choate (ed.) *Successful Inclusive Teaching* (2nd edn). Boston: Allyn and Bacon.

Minton, P. (1992) Using the computer to help dyslexics study words and master spelling. *Australian Journal of Remedial Education*, 24, 4, 12-14.

Moats, L.C. (1995) *Spelling: Development, Disability and Instruction*. Baltimore: York Press.

Moseley, D. (1997) Assessment of spelling and related aspects of written expression. In J.R. Beech and C. Singleton (eds) *The Psychological Assessment of Reading*. London: Routledge.

Nichols, R. (1985) *Helping Your Child Spell*. Earley: University of Reading.

Nicholson, T. (1994) *At the Cutting Edge: Recent Research on Learning to Read and Spell*. Wellington: New Zealand Council for Educational Research.

O'Flahavan, J.F. and Blassberg, R. (1992) Toward an embedded model of spelling instruction for emergent literates. *Language Arts*, 69, 6, 409-417.

Padget, S.Y., Knight, D.F. and Sawyer, D.J. (1996) Tennessee meets the challenge of dyslexia. *Annals of Dyslexia*, 46, 51-72.

Parker, R. (1991) Spelling at home. In V. Nicoll and L. Wilkie (eds) *Literacy at Home and School*. Rozell, NSW: Primary English Teaching Association.

Peters, M.L. (1974a) The significance of spelling miscues. In B. Wade and K. Wedell (eds) *Spelling: Task and Learner*. Birmingham: University of Birmingham Press.

Peters, M.L. (1974b) Teacher variables in spelling. In B. Wade and K. Wedell (eds) *Spelling: Task and Learner*. Birmingham: University of Birmingham Press.

Peters, M.L. (1975) *Diagnostic and Remedial Spelling Manual*. London: Macmillan.

Peters, M.L (1985) *Spelling: Caught or Taught? A New Look*. London: Routledge.

Peters, M.L. and Cripps, C. (1980) *Catchwords: Ideas for Teaching Spelling* (2nd edn). Sydney: Harcourt Brace Jovanovich.

Peters, M.L. and Smith, B. (1993) *Spelling in Context*. Windsor: NFER-Nelson.

Polloway, E.A. and Patton. J.R. (1997) *Strategies for Teaching Learners with Special Needs* (6th edn). Upper Saddle River, NJ: Merrill.

Pumfrey, P. and Reason, R. (1991) *Specific Learning Difficulties: Dyslexia*. London: Routledge.

Ralston, M. and Robinson, G. (1997) Spelling strategies and metacognitive awareness in skilled and unskilled spellers. *Australian Journal of Learning Disabilities*, *2*, *4*, 12-23.

Read, C. and Hodges, R.E. (1982) Spelling. In H.E. Mitzel, J.H. Best and W. Rabinowitz (eds) *Encyclopedia of Educational Research* (5th edn). London: Collier Macmillan.

Reason, R. and Boote, R. (1994) *Helping Children with Reading and Spelling*. London: Routledge.

Redfern, A. (1993) *Practical Ways to Teach Spelling*. Reading: University of Reading.

Rohl, M. and Tunmer, W. (1988) Phonemic segmentation skill and spelling acquisition. *Applied Psycholinguistics*, *9*, *4*, 335-350.

Rowe, G. and Lomas, B. (1996) *Systematic Spelling: A Classroom Action Plan*. Burwood: Dellasta.

Salend, S. (1994) *Effective Mainstreaming* (2nd edn). New York: Macmillan.

Schonell, F.J. (1958) *Essentials in Teaching and Testing Spelling*. London: Macmillan.

Sears, H.C. and Johnson, D.M. (1986) The effects of visual imagery on spelling performance. *Journal of Educational Research*, *79*, *4*, 230-233.

Snowball, D. (1997a) Spelling strategies, *Classroom*, *17*, *2*, 20-21

Snowball, D. (1997b) Spelling: learning high frequency words. *Classroom*, *17*, *3*, 18-19.

Snowball, D. (1997c) Fun spelling games for serious skill building. *Instructor*, *106*, 7, 28-29.

Stewart, S.R. and Cegelka, P.T. (1995) Teaching reading and spelling. In P.T. Cegelka and W.H. Berdine (eds) *Effective Instruction for Students with Learning Difficulties*. Boston: Allyn and Bacon.

Tangel, D.M. and Blachman, B.A. (1995) Effect of phoneme awareness instruction on the invented spelling of first-grade children: a one-year follow up. *Journal of Reading Behaviour*, *27*, *2*, 153-185.

Templeton, S. (1992) New trends in an historic perspective: old story, new resolution— sound and meaning in spelling. *Language Arts*, *69*, *6*, 454-463.

Thomson, M. (1995) Evaluating teaching programs for children with specific learning difficulties. *Australian Journal of Remedial Education*, *27*, *1*, 20-27.

Thurstone, L.L. (1948) Psychological implications of factor analysis. *American Psychologist*, *3*, 402-408.

Varnhagen, C.K., Varnhagen, S. and Das, J.P. (1992) Analysis of cognitive processing and spelling errors of average and reading-disabled children. *Reading Psychology*, *13*, *3*, 217-239.

Vaughn, S., Bos, C.S. and Schumm, J.S. (1997) *Teaching Mainstreamed, Diverse, and At-Risk Students in the General Education Classroom*. Boston: Allyn and Bacon.

Vincent, D. and Claydon, J. (1982) *Diagnostic Spelling Test* (Australian edn, 1996). Coldstream, Victoria: Professional Resources Services.

5317

Waring, S., Prior, M., Sanson, A. and Smart, D. (1996) Predictors of recovery from reading disability. *Australian Journal of Psychology, 48, 3*, 160-166.

Watkins, G. and Hunter-Carsch, M. (1995) Prompt spelling: a practical approach to paired spelling. *Support for Learning, 10, 3*, 133-137.

Weckert, C. (1989) *Spelling Companion for Teachers*. Sydney: Horwitz-Grahame.

Westwood, P.S. (1973) Predicting expressive and receptive language performance from measures of psycholinguistic ability. Unpublished Masters Degree thesis, University of Manchester.

Westwood, P.S. (1979) *Helping Children with Spelling Difficulties*. Adelaide: Education Department of South Australia.

Westwood, P.S. (1994) Issues in spelling instruction. *Special Education Perspectives, 3, 1*, 31-44.

Westwood, P.S. (1997) *Commonsense Methods for Children with Special Needs* (3rd edn). London: Routledge.

Westwood, P.S. (1999) The correlation between results from different types of spelling test and children's spelling ability while writing, *Australian Journal of Learning Disabilities, 5, 1* [In press].

Wirtz, C.L., Gardner, R., Weber, K. and Bullara, D. (1996) Using self-correction to improve the spelling performance of low-achieving third graders. *Remedial and Special Education, 17, 1*, 48-58.

Wong, B. (1986) A cognitive approach to teaching spelling. *Exceptional Children, 53*, 169-173.

Zutell, J. (1998) Word sorting: a developmental spelling approach to word study for delayed readers. *Reading and Writing Quarterly, 14, 2*, 219-238.

Index

analogy
  as a spelling strategy 5, 20, 27, 48
attitudes
  importance of in spelling 25
automaticity 12, 14, 15, 26, 49
benchmarks for spelling 43, 46-7
computers
  role in spelling 13, 20, 38-9, 42
correction of errors 3, 36
curriculum-based assessment 50
developmental stages in spelling 7-11, 20, 44, 46, 55, 57
diagnosis in spelling 11-12, 43-52
diagnostic testing 50-1, 52, 70-2
Directed Spelling Thinking Activity (DSTA) 34-5, 40
dual coding system 15
dyslexia 2, 19, 21, 22, 40
English Profiles 47-8, 64
error analysis
  as a diagnostic procedure 44-5, 57
  difficulties associated with 45
error correction 3, 36
error imitation 34, 42
explicit teaching 1, 5, 7, 19, 23, 26, 28, 31
First Steps 47, 57
generalisation in learning
  difficulties with 3, 5, 36
  the need to facilitate 22, 28-9, 34, 38, 58
grapho-phonic knowledge (see also phonic knowledge) 17, 19, 26, 29, 34, 35-6, 48, 71-2
handwriting 14, 56, 58
high-frequency words 25, 26, 32, 37, 42, 44, 45, 48, 63
incidental learning 1, 4, 17, 23
invented spelling 8, 12, 32, 48
keyboard skills 32, 42
kinaesthetic memory 13-14, 16, 32
learning difficulties 7, 20-1, 33, 35, 38, 41-2, 48, 51, 71

learning disability 2, 19, 21, 22, 34, 40, 45
letter strings
  importance of knowledge of 9, 10, 14, 15, 17, 21, 26, 27, 28, 30, 35, 49
lists 2, 5, 35-6, 63
long-term memory 3, 13, 14, 32, 40, 42
look-cover-write-check strategy 30-1, 37
mini lessons 28
mnemonics 14, 20
morphemic principles 9, 14, 16, 19, 21-2, 27, 36, 38, 49, 59
Morphographic Spelling 27, 28, 59
motor memory 14, 15, 32
Old Way-New Way strategy 33-4
onset-rime 26, 48, 61
overlearning 21, 38
parents 2, 3, 37, 55
peer tutoring 36-7, 42
phonemic awareness 11, 12, 20, 21, 22, 26, 40, 61
phonemic strategy 5, 22
phonetic stage of development 8-9, 12, 26, 30, 41
phonic knowledge 8, 16, 21, 26, 35-6, 48, 62, 71-2
phonological awareness 12, 17, 21, 26
portfolios 45-6, 53
prefixes 27, 36
pre-phonemic stage 7-8, 22, 39, 41
proactive inhibition 33
Prompt Spelling method 36-7
proofreading 10, 20, 37, 39-40, 44, 49, 52, 59
reading-spelling connection 16-17, 39, 56
repeated writing strategy 32-3, 40
resources for spelling instruction 55-9
rote learning 3, 5, 32, 37
self-assessment 46, 53
self-correction 10, 38, 44, 47, 49, 52
self-monitoring 19, 42, 44

simultaneous oral spelling (SOS) 33, 40
South Australian Spelling Test (SAST) 52, 64-69
speech and spelling 12, 45, 56
spell-checkers 13, 20, 38-39
spelling
  across the curriculum 1, 2
  benchmarks 46-7
  'demons' 37, 53, 55, 71
  developmental stages 7-11, 46
  diagnostic assessment 11-12, 70-2
  differing views on 1-2
  outcomes and indicators 48-9
  stages of development 7-11, 20, 46
  teaching approaches 2-42
  testing 50-2, 56-8, 70-2
spelling lists 35, 37-8
Spelling Mastery 28, 58
strategies
  assessment of 11, 43
  importance of for spelling 5-6, 11, 15, 19, 20, 23, 30, 49
  teaching 29-32
suffixes 21, 36
Teaching Handwriting, Reading and Spelling Skills (THRASS) 27, 28, 56-7
testing 42, 50-2, 56-8
transitional stage of development 9-10, 26, 27, 40, 41
tutorial help 36-7
visual attention span (VAS) 30
visual imagery 5, 13, 20, 22, 30-2, 40, 41, 49
whole language approach 3-5, 28, 31-2
word families 21, 35-6
word lists 5, 35-6, 63, 70
word processors 38-9
Word Sorts 35, 40
word study
  activities for 27, 28, 34-6
  importance of 4, 17, 19, 25-6